Google Explored

Books Available

By the same authors:

BP595	Google Explored
BP590	Microsoft Access 2007 explained
BP585	Microsoft Excel 2007 explained
BP584	Microsoft Word 2007 explained
BP583	Microsoft Office 2007 explained
BP581	Windows Vista explained
BP580	Windows Vista for Beginners
BP569	Microsoft Works 8.0 & Works Suite 2006 explained
BP563	Using Windows XP's Accessories
BP558	Microsoft Works 8.0 & Works Suite 2005 explained
BP557	How Did I Do That ... in Windows XP
BP555	Using PDF Files
BP550	Advanced Guide to Windows XP
BP548	Easy PC Keyboard Shortcuts
BP546	Microsoft Works Suite 2004 explained
BP545	Paint Shop Pro 8 explained
BP544	Microsoft Office 2003 explained
BP538	Windows XP for Beginners
BP525	Controlling Windows XP the easy way
BP522	Microsoft Works Suite 2002 explained
BP514	Windows XP explained
BP513	IE 6 and Outlook Express 6 explained
BP512	Microsoft Access 2002 explained
BP511	Microsoft Excel 2002 explained
BP510	Microsoft Word 2002 explained
BP509	Microsoft Office XP explained
BP498	Using Visual Basic
BP493	Windows Me explained
BP491	Windows 2000 explained
BP487	Quicken 2000 UK explained
BP486	Using Linux the easy way
BP465	Lotus SmartSuite Millennium explained
BP433	Your own Web site on the Internet
BP341	MS-DOS explained
BP284	Programming in QuickBASIC
BP258	Learning to Program in C

Google Explored

by

P.R.M. Oliver
and
N. Kantaris

Bernard Babani (publishing) Ltd
The Grampians
Shepherds Bush Road
London W6 7NF
England
www.babanibooks.com

Please Note

Although every care has been taken with the production of this book to ensure that any projects, designs, modifications and/or programs, etc., contained herewith, operate in a correct and safe manner and also that any components specified are normally available in Great Britain, the Publishers and Author(s) do not accept responsibility in any way for the failure (including fault in design) of any project, design, modification or program to work correctly or to cause damage to any equipment that it may be connected to or used in conjunction with, or in respect of any other damage or injury that may be so caused, nor do the Publishers accept responsibility in any way for the failure to obtain specified components.

Notice is also given that if equipment that is still under warranty is modified in any way or used or connected with home-built equipment then that warranty may be void.

First Published – November 2008

British Library Cataloguing in Publication Data:

A catalogue record for this book is available from the British Library

ISBN 978 0 85934 595 8

Cover Design by Gregor Arthur
Printed and Bound in Great Britain by J.H. Haynes & Co. Ltd.

About this Book

Google

These days we all use simple Google searches when we are on the Internet, to such an extent that to 'google' is now an accepted English verb. But Google is much more than just a search tool, as this book explains.

Google Explored has been written to help you use Google Search more effectively, and to explore many of the other applications and tools offered by Google. Chapters include:

- Introducing **Google** as a company, using **Web Search** and how to make online shopping quick and easy with Google **Product Search** and Google **Checkout**.

- Installing and using the **Google Toolbar** to add new functions to your Explorer or Firefox Web browsers, and how to AutoFill forms on Web pages.

- Using **Google News** to easily keep abreast of World and local news as and when it happens, as well as searching and exploring historical news archives.

- Using **Google Finance** to get instant up to date and historical data on stocks and shares, mutual funds, foreign currencies and public companies.

- Carrying out all your E-mailing with **Google Mail**, creating, organising and sharing your documents, spreadsheets and presentations by 'cloud computing' with **Google Docs**, and how to organise your life with the **Google Calendar**.

- Organising, editing and sharing your digital photos with **Picasa**.

- Watching videos, searching for them, or displaying your own videos on the Internet with **YouTube**.

- Using **Google Maps** to view maps and local business information, get driving, walking and public transport directions, get traffic information, view satellite imagery and walk through Street View of some parts of the World.

- Flying with **Google Earth** to anywhere on the globe and viewing satellite imagery, maps, terrain, Street View, 3D buildings and even explore galaxies in **Sky,** and nearer to home, the Moon.

- Finally a chapter is included giving a comprehensive introduction to Google's new Web browser, **Google Chrome**.

One of the exciting things about writing this book was the speed with which things change with Google. Nothing seems to stay the same for long. Programs were added and changed all the way through. Where possible we have included the changes here. Their Web logo changed several times during this period, see **G1** in Colour Gallery 1 to see the one they used to commemorate their 10th birthday.

Google Explored was written with the busy person in mind. We all are these days, and it's not necessary to learn all there is to know about a subject, when reading a few selected pages will cover it adequately.

Using this book, it is hoped that you will be able to enjoy the Google tools and applications we have covered and get the most out of your computer in terms of efficiency, productivity and enjoyment. Good luck and have fun.

About the Authors

Phil Oliver graduated in Mining Engineering at Camborne School of Mines in 1967 and since then has specialised in most aspects of surface mining technology, with a particular emphasis on computer related techniques. He has worked in Guyana, Canada, several Middle Eastern and Asian countries, South Africa and the United Kingdom, on such diverse projects as: the planning and management of bauxite, iron, gold and coal mines; rock excavation contracting in the UK; international mining equipment sales and international mine consulting. In 1988 he took up a lecturing position at Camborne School of Mines (part of Exeter University) in Surface Mining and Management. He retired from this in 1998, to spend more time writing, consulting and developing Web sites for clients.

Noel Kantaris graduated in Electrical Engineering at Bristol University and after spending three years in the Electronics Industry in London, took up a Tutorship in Physics at the University of Queensland. Research interests in Ionospheric Physics, led to the degrees of M.E. in Electronics and Ph.D. in Physics. On return to the UK, he took up a Post-Doctoral Research Fellowship in Radio Physics at the University of Leicester, and then in 1973 a lecturing position in Engineering at the Camborne School of Mines, Cornwall, (part of Exeter University), where between 1978 and 1997 he was also the CSM IT Manager. At present he is IT Director of FFC Ltd.

Acknowledgements

We would like to thank friends and colleagues, for their helpful tips and suggestions which assisted us in the writing of this book.

Trademarks

Contents

Point of Interest

While we were preparing this book, Google launched their new Web browser (see Chapter 15), and called it **Google Chrome**. We thought this was an unusual name, so we did some research and found it was nothing to do with the metal chromium.

Apparently, in software development, **chrome** refers to the frame of an application – the toolbars, title bars and buttons that surround the working area. With their new browser, Google wanted to eliminate as much of this 'chrome' as possible, to give a simpler, cleaner, more professional design. They came up with the mantra "content, not chrome" as one of their main guiding principles behind the design.

It's not hard to see how **Chrome** came to the fore, when they eventually came to choose a name for the browser.

1

About Google

Google, arguably the most popular search engine on the Internet, is a tool for finding resources on the World Wide Web. At some time, everyone that uses the Internet probably uses simple Google searches to find what they are looking for. We have been using them since it first 'went public' in the late 1990s.

But Google is much more than just a search tool, as this book sets out to explain. Google is about organising the world's knowledge. It maintains indexes of Web pages and other online content such as images, movies, books, business information, news, maps, scholarly papers, videos and music, and makes this information freely available to anyone with an Internet connection, as shown in G3.

To pay for all this, Google generates its income mainly by delivering unobtrusive online advertising on its search results pages.

The Name

The name "Google" originated from a misspelling of "googol" the unimaginably large number 10^{100}, (the digit 1 followed by a hundred zeros in decimal representation). The term was coined in 1938 by Milton Sirotta the nine year old nephew of American mathematician Edward Kasner, who used the concept in his book *Mathematics and the Imagination*. Google's play on the term reflects the company's mission to organise the immense amount of information available on the Internet.

An Interesting History

Google began in January 1996 as a research project by Larry Page, a Ph.D. student at Stanford University. For his thesis he focused on the problem of finding out which Web pages link to any given page, considering the number and nature of such backlinks to be valuable information about that page. He nicknamed this project 'BackRub', and was soon joined by Sergey Brin, a fellow Stanford Ph.D. student and close friend. Their Web crawler began exploring the Web in March 1996, setting out from their own Stanford home page as its only starting point. To convert the backlink data that it gathered into a measure of importance for a given Web page, Brin and Page developed the PageRank algorithm.

Convinced that the pages with the most links to them from other highly relevant Web pages must be the most relevant pages associated with a Web search, Page and Brin tested their thesis as part of their studies, and laid the foundation for their search engine. It proved successful and Brin and Page put their studies on hold and raised $1 million from family, friends and other investors. In September 1998 Google was incorporated in a garage with four employees. At that time it was getting 10,000 search queries per day.

Because it was easy to use and produced very rapid relevant search results, Google rapidly became very popular and expanded at enormous speed. While the 'dotcom' boom exploded around it, Google focused on building a better search engine. In 1999 AOL selected Google as a search partner, and Yahoo followed suit a year later.

Google shares were offered to the public for the first time in August 2004 at a price of US$85 per share, but the vast majority of the 271 million shares offered stayed under Google's control, and many of their employees became instant paper millionaires.

Google shares reached US$700 in October 2007, but are considerably lower at the time of writing. On 30 June 2008 Google had 19,604 employees, and a market valuation of US$179 Billion. Not bad going in just over 10 years!

Company Overview

Google's published mission is to organise the world's information and make it universally accessible and useful on the Internet. Co-founder Larry Page's aim is to create a perfect search engine that, "understands exactly what you mean and gives you back exactly what you want".

The software behind Google's search technology conducts a series of simultaneous calculations requiring only a fraction of a second. It uses *PageRank* to examine the entire link structure of the Web and determine which pages are most important. It then conducts a text matching analysis to determine which pages are relevant to a specific search.

Google is now widely recognised as the world's largest search engine, which is an easy-to-use free service that usually returns relevant results in a fraction of a second.

Google's search success and its ease of use have made it one of the world's best known brands almost entirely through word of mouth from users. Having found its way increasingly into everyday language the verb 'google', was added to the Oxford English Dictionary in 2006, meaning, "to use the Google search engine to obtain information on the Internet".

As a business, Google generates revenue by providing advertisers with the opportunity to deliver measurable, cost-effective online advertising that is relevant to the search information displayed on any given page. The advertising is usually so relevant that it is actually useful to the searcher. It is always labelled as advertising so is easy to distinguish from the search results or other page contents.

Searching with Google is so simple, efficient and effective that it's easy to take it for granted and to hardly notice it's there. But it's hard to imagine life without it.

Just how big is the Internet? Well, if anyone should know it would probably be Google. They announced in July 2008 that they now search and index over 1 trillion Web sites (1,000,000,000,000). Wow, but the number of individual Web pages out there is growing by several billion per day!

Cloud Computing

Lately you may have been hearing in the media about "cloud computing" or using Web-based software to work on your data and files, and storing them online instead of on your hard drive. Doing so gives you the freedom to access your documents and photos anywhere you have Internet access, from any computer – especially helpful when you are travelling.

'The Cloud' is a metaphor for the Internet, and cloud computing often eliminates the need to install and run software applications on your own computer, reducing the burden of software maintenance, updating, and support.

Pretty well all of the Google tools we cover in this book are based online, but the cloud computing concept applies particularly to Google's Docs, Calendar, Maps and Gmail, that let you access your data through your Web browser.

It's not so long ago that we both used large computer based mapping and atlas programs that needed updating frequently as our environment changed. Now we get far better, and free, coverage from Microsoft's and Google's online based mapping tools.

The cloud is great for sharing data as well. With Google Docs you can invite people to contribute to your document just by sending them a link.

The cloud concept can raise concerns about privacy and loss of control over sensitive data. Performance can also be affected by insufficient bandwidth or high network loads. But overall, the device and location independence enabling you to access systems wherever you are must outweigh these concerns. They do for us, anyway.

Technology Overview

Search engines, like Google, carry out three main operations.

Crawling – The process by which Googlebot, Google's robot or spider, discovers new and updated pages to be added to the Google index. As Googlebot visits Web sites it detects the links on each page and adds them to its list of pages to crawl. New sites, changes to existing sites, and dead links are noted and used to update the index.

Indexing – Googlebot scans the pages it crawls and builds an index of all the words it sees and their location on each page.

Serving results – When a user enters a query, Google searches the index for matching pages and returns a list of links to the pages it considers most relevant. Over 200 factors are considered, including PageRank.

As well as the Web page search service, Google also runs a number of vertical search services, such as:

Google News.
Google News Archive.
Google Book Search.
Google Scholar, an academic search program.
Google Blog Search.
Google Base, a database of uploaded information describing online or offline content, products, or services.
Google Images.
Google Video.

Google now mixes search results from these vertical services into their organic search results.

A Google Query

The life span of a Google query normally lasts less than half a second, yet involves a number of different steps that must be completed before results can be delivered to the person seeking the information, as shown in colour illustration G2.

- The query is checked to match any advanced syntax and if it is spelled incorrectly a more popular or correct spelling variation is flagged.

- A check is made to see if the query is relevant to the other vertical search databases listed earlier, and relevant links are chosen to go with the regular search results.

- In the Index Servers a list of relevant pages for the organic search result is prepared and ranked on page content, usage and link data.

- A list of relevant adverts is chosen for placement near the search results.

- The query then travels to Google's Doc Servers, which actually retrieve the stored documents and generates short snippets describing each search result.

- Finally the search results are returned to the user in a fraction of a second.

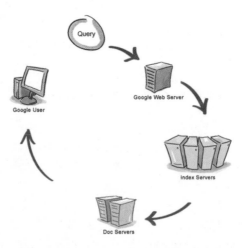

Fig. 1.1 The Life of a Simple Google Query

2

Searching the Web

Web Searches

As you all know, doing a search on Google is easy, but with a little more knowledge, you can get much more from Google. For a basic search in the UK, open the Google UK home page (see **G4**) by typing **www.google.co.uk** into your browser's Address Bar, as shown below.

Fig. 2.1 Google Search Home Page

Then simply type the words, or phrase, that best describes the information you want to find into the **Search Box** and press the **Enter** key, or click the **Google Search** button.

If you have an up to date Web browser the **Instant Search** box lets you search the Web directly from the Address bar, as shown in Fig. 2.1. Just type your search query into this box. You may have to change the settings in the drop-down menu (open on the previous page) to set Google as the search tool used. Microsoft like you to use their own search engine!

Fig. 2.2 Google Search Results Page

Google produces a results page, like the one shown in Fig. 2.2 above, with a list of Web pages related to your search terms. It ranks the list with what it considers the most relevant match found at the top. Clicking any underlined link in the results list will take you to the related Web page.

Note that in our example, Google recognised our spelling mistake, and searched for *dolphins*, not *dolfins*. Clever stuff.

The Search Results Page

The results page contains lots of information about the search. Here we show and describe the parts of the page, starting from the top, and working from left to right.

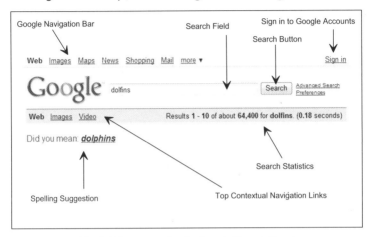

Fig. 2.3 Components of a Google Search Page

Google Navigation Bar – Click the link for the Google service you want to use. You can search the Web, browse for images, maps, news, shopping, navigate to Gmail or click on **More** to access other Google products.

Sign in to Google Accounts – Sign in to, or open, your Google Account. This lets you customise pages, view recommendations, and get more relevant search results.

Search Field – The text box where you type your search terms to start a Google search.

Search Button – Click this button to send a search query. This is the same as pressing the **Enter** key.

Advanced Search – This links to a page on which you can do more precise searches.

Preferences – This links to a page that lets you set your search preferences, such as language, results per page, and screening to avoid getting adult material.

Top Contextual Navigation Links – Dynamic links which suggest content types relevant to your search. You can click them to see more results of a particular content type.

Search Statistics – This describes your search, indicating the total number of results, and how long the search took to complete (0.18 seconds in our example).

Spelling Suggestion – If Google thinks you made a mistake entering your query, it will suggest another search term, depending on where you are located. It is quite intuitive and recognises that different terms and spelling are used in different parts of the world.

YouTube - Dolphins off the Isles of Scilly, **Cornwall** ...
Dolphins off the isle of St Martin, in the Isles of Scilly ...
47 sec - ✰✰✰✰✰
www.youtube.com/watch?v=1Kce1OHE3ck

Dolphins- Newquay **Cornwall**
the **Cornish** Dolphin Project was set up by the Whale and Dolphin Conservation Society to study the dolphins in detail. Contact the **Cornwall** Wildlife Trust ...
www.newquayguide.co.uk/dolphins.html - 8k - Cached - Similar pages

Fig. 2.4 Search Results from Different Content Types

Google's search results are integrated and can be made up of multiple content types, such as images, news, books, maps and videos. It searches across all of these content sources, integrates and then ranks the results for the best answers. Fig. 2.4 shows a video and a Web page from a set of results.

Page Title – The first line of any search result item is the title of the Web page found. If there is a URL instead then the Web page has no title.

Text below the Title – This is an excerpt from the results page with the query terms boldened.

URL of Result – This gives the Web address of the result.

Size – This number (8k in our example above) is the size of the text portion of the Web page, and gives an idea of how quickly the resulting page will display.

Cached – Clicking this link will show you the contents of the Web page when we last indexed it.

Similar Pages – When you click this link Google will search for other pages that are related to this result.

Related Search Terms – Sometimes Google can suggest better search terms than the ones you actually entered. You can then click these related search terms to see alternate search results.

About Search Terms

With Google, choosing the right search terms is the key to finding the information you need. It is often better to use multiple search terms. If you're planning a vacation in Cornwall, you may do better searching for **vacation cornwall** than with the words by themselves. And if you are interested in fishing, then **vacation cornwall fishing** may produce even better results. Choose your search terms carefully as Google can only look for what you choose.

Google searches are **NOT** case sensitive. All letters, regardless of how you type them, will be understood as lower case, so there is no point using capitals (as shown above).

By default, Google only returns pages that include all of your search terms, and the order in which the terms are typed will affect the search results. To restrict a search further, just include more terms.

Google ignores common words and characters such as "in" and "how", and single digits and letters, because they slow down a search without improving the results. If a common word is essential to getting the results you want, you can include it by putting a "+" sign in front of it, but make sure there is a space before the "+".

Another method for doing this is conducting a phrase search and putting quotation marks "" around two or more words. Common words in a phrase search, such as "where are you" are included in the search. Phrase searches are also effective when searching for specific phrases such as in names, song lyrics or poems.

I'm Feeling Lucky

You can force Google to go straight to what it considers the most relevant Web site for your query. To do this, enter your search terms on the Google home page as usual, but click the **I'm Feeling Lucky** button, instead of the **Google Search** button, as shown in Fig. 2.1. We must admit that we don't use this feature very often.

Google Search File Types

As well as normal Web documents formatted in HTML, there are 13 other file types that Google indexes when it crawls the Web. These are:

Adobe Portable Document Format (pdf)
Adobe PostScript (ps)
Text (ans, txt)
Microsoft Word (doc)
Microsoft Excel (xls)
Microsoft PowerPoint (ppt)
Microsoft Works (wks, wps, wdb)
Microsoft Write (wri)
Lotus 1-2-3 (wk1, wk2, wk3, wk4, wk5, wki, wks, wku)
Lotus WordPro (lwp)
MacWrite (mw)
Rich Text Format (rtf)
Shockwave Flash (swf)

The first four file types listed are fairly common, with the others by comparison being less common.

In a search result the file format is usually indicated with blue text in brackets in front of the page title. This lets you know that a viewer for the program in which the file was created is needed to display the file. However Google converts all file types it searches to either HTML or text. The search results include links to either **View as HTML** or **View as Text**, which gives you faster access to the file and means you don't need the original application.

Advanced Searching

This offers options for making your searches more precise and is opened by clicking the **Advanced Search** link on the Google home page, shown in Fig. 2.1.

Fig. 2.5 Google's Advanced Search Box

Here you can search only for pages:

- that contain ALL the search terms you type in.
- that contain the exact phrase you type in.
- that contain at least one of the words you type in.
- that do NOT contain any of the words you type in.
- written in a certain language.
- created in a certain file format.
- that have been updated within a certain period of time.
- that contain numbers within a certain range.
- within a certain domain, or Web site.
- that don't contain "adult" material.

When you have a few minutes to spare we suggest you have a play with this Advanced Search box. After a while you should be able to fine tune your searches and save a lot of time.

If you click the three **Tip** options to the right of the text entry boxes, you will see how you can get the same results in the Google search box, by adding search "operators", such as "", **OR** or the minus sign –.

Some Advanced Operators

These more advanced operators can help narrow down your search results.

Intitle: When placed at the beginning of a query this restricts your search results to just the titles of Web pages. The search **intitle:"fred blogs"** for instance returns pages with **fred blogs** in their titles.

Intext: This does the opposite – only the body text is searched, ignoring titles and links.

Link: This lets you see which pages are linked to the page you're interested in. For example, the query **link:http://www.philoliver.com** shows who has linked to one of our own Web sites!

Site:	Used to search a specific Web site for content that matches a certain phrase. The query **babani site:philoliver.com** searches for references to our publisher on one of our sites. This lets you search a site that does not have its own search facilities.
Define:	Produces a list of definitions from different linked sources. Try the query **define:egg** to see what we mean.
~	To search not only for your search term but also for its synonyms, or things that mean the same, you can place the tilde sign ~ immediately in front of your search term.
Related:	To search for Web pages that have similar content to a given site, type "related:" followed by the site address into the search box.

Special Search Features

In addition to providing easy access to billions of Web pages, Google Web Search has many special features that most people don't seem to know about. With these, the feature result appears at the top of the list of Web page results.

Some of the features only apply to the USA, but some of our most popular and useful ones here in the UK are listed below. Please bear in mind though, that Google is always in a state of flux. New features are added quite often and by the time you read this, there may be many more of them.

Weather

To see the weather for most UK towns and cities, type **weather** followed by the town name. Sometimes a county or postcode is needed as well. For a colour example see **G5**.

Fig. 2.6 Getting an Instant Local Weather Forecast

Time

To see the current time in most cities of the world, type in **time** and the name of the city, as we did for Sydney in Fig. 2.7 below.

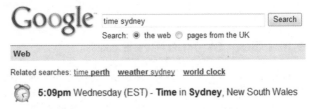

Fig. 2.7 An Instant World Time Clock

If you type just **time** you will get the current time for wherever you are.

Movies

If you want to go to the cinema, Google is the first place to look. Just type **cinema** followed by the name of your town into the Google search box, and click the **Search** button. You should get a result like ours in Fig. 2.8, listing the cinemas in the town alongside a map of their location, and giving details of the films being shown. Clicking the **Showtimes for...** link will give you details of starting times, etc.

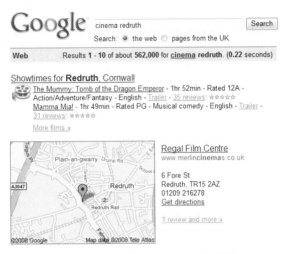

Fig. 2.8 Finding What Movies are on and Where

To find cinemas and 'showtimes' near you for a currently playing film, simply search for the film's name and enter the location details in the **Town or post code** box, as shown in Fig. 2.9 below.

Fig. 2.9 Searching for a Particular Film

If you have already saved your location on a previous search, that location will be used again by default.

As can be seen above, the search results for a film include a star rating (out of 5), snippets from online reviews, as well as links to the reviews themselves, and to trailers for the film. More than enough information to plan your evening!

Airline Travel Information

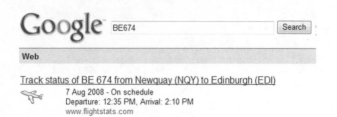

Fig. 2.10 Finding Current Flight Information

To check the flight status for international or domestic flights just type the flight number (such as BE674) into the search box, as shown above, and click on **Search**. This can be very useful if you have to meet an incoming flight. If you click the **Track status...** link you can track the full details of the flight in real time on the FlightStats Web site.

Google Q&A

Sometimes entering a simple question into Google, such as '**height of mount everest**' or '**when was tony blair born**' will come up with the answer at the top of the results page. With the latter this was:

Tony Blair — Date of Birth: 6 May 1953.

Currency Conversion

Google has a built-in currency converter, so if you are going to Greece on vacation and want to take 1200 Euros with you, simply enter the conversion **1200 euros in pounds** into the search box and click on **Search**. The last time we did this the answer on the results page was:

 1 200 Euros = 942.297155 British pounds

Fig. 2.11 A Currency Conversion Result

You don't get much for your pounds these days! If you don't know the currency of your target, just enter a simple **Q&A** into the Google search box, like **currency of turkey**, and then use the result (Turkish lira) for the conversion.

Local Business Searches

If you're looking for a store, restaurant, or other local business or service you can search for the category of business and the location and Google will return your information on the results page, with a map, reviews, and contact information, as shown below for our search **pizza truro cornwall**. Sometimes you have to add the county as well as the town, to get this to work.

Fig. 2.12 Results of a Typical Local Business Search

Spell Checker

Fig. 2.13 Spell Checking

Google checks whether any query you enter uses the most common spelling of a given word. If it thinks you're likely to generate better results with an alternative (or more correct) spelling, it will ask '**Did you mean:**', as shown here in Fig. 2.13. Clicking the underlined suggestion starts a Google search for that term.

Maps

If you need a quick map to find a location or post code, just type in the name of the location, or post code, followed by '**map**' and Google will return a small map of the location.

Fig. 2.14 Generating a Quick Map – See **G6** for a Colour Version

Clicking on the map will take you to a much more detailed version in Google Maps, which is described in Chapter 13.

Cricket Scores

Not many people know that Google Search has a feature which shows the live cricket scores of important matches currently being, or recently, played. To see this, just enter **cricket** in the Google Search box and press **Enter**.

Fig. 2.15 Getting Cricket Results

The scorecard is very brief, but clicking the match link opens a full scorecard. Why this operates for cricket and not the other main British sports we don't know. Perhaps the programming was done in India.

Book Search

 Google have scanned an enormous number of books into digital format and by entering the name of an author or a book title into the Google search box you can access their Book Search feature.

Fig. 2.16 Entering Google Book Search

In Fig. 2.16 above we have searched for **thomas hardy** and have been given three examples of his books. Clicking the **Books by...** link opens a full listing of the author's work.

You can click on an item to view more detailed information about the author or title. Clicking on a book title shows basic details of the book which might include a few snippets of text.

If a publisher or author has given Google permission, you should see a full page and be able to browse the book to see more pages.

If the book is out of copyright, you can page forward or backward through the full book. Clicking on **Search within this book** lets you carry out more searches within the book.

Clicking a link in the **Buy this Book** section links you to an online bookstore where you can buy the book.

Calculator

Google Web Search includes another special feature which we think deserves a small section of its own, the calculator. This does not have a front-end, as you might expect, you just type your maths problem straight into the search box and get instant answers. As long as you have your browser open to the Internet it is always just a click away. The calculator will even recognise words as well as numbers.

The entries **nine plus six minus four**, or **9 plus 6 minus 4**, or **9+6-4**, all give the answer of 11.

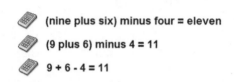

(nine plus six) minus four = eleven

(9 plus 6) minus 4 = 11

9 + 6 - 4 = 11

Fig. 2.17 Entering Numbers or Text into the Calculator

This very powerful feature lets you perform simple as well complex calculations using Google's search box. It can solve problems involving basic arithmetic, units of measure, conversions, and physical constants.

As well as text you can use the usual operators, **+** for addition, **–** for subtraction, ***** for multiplication, **/** for division, and **^** for exponentiation, or raising to the power of. In Fig. 2.18 we show how trigonometric functions can very easily be used.

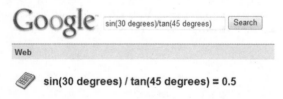

Google   sin(30 degrees)/tan(45 degrees)   Search

Web

sin(30 degrees) / tan(45 degrees) = 0.5

Fig. 2.18 Using Trigonometric Functions in the Calculator

Making Conversions

One of the things that makes the Google calculator so useful for us is its ability to make conversions between types of units. As long as you label them, you can use mixed units in a query and even get your results converted to something else. The terminology for conversions is:

(old units) in (new units)

The example in Fig. 2.19 below shows the use of automatic and forced conversions in the calculator.

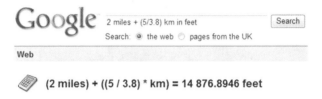

(2 miles) + ((5 / 3.8) * km) = 14 876.8946 feet

Fig. 2.19 A Calculation Using Mixed Units

The numbering systems that can be used with the calculator include decimal, hexadecimal or hex, octal, binary, and even Roman numerals.

If you are interested in Roman history you have at last found an easy way to convert to and from Roman numerals.

1976 = MCMLXXVI

Fig. 2.20 Converting a Decimal Number to Roman Numerals

A more complete listing of the calculator functions is given in Appendix A. This is really an excellent feature and we strongly recommend you experiment with it.

Searching for Pictures

To use Google to search for images, such as photographs, icons, drawings and maps on the Web you can use Image Search. This gives you access to billions of indexed pictures which are available for viewing.

To use Image Search, select **Images** on the Google Navigation Bar as pointed to in Fig. 2.21 below, and enter your query in the **Search** box, then click on the **Search Images** button.

Fig. 2.21 Starting an Image Search

Here we are searching the Web again for **dolphins**, but this time we want pictures of them.

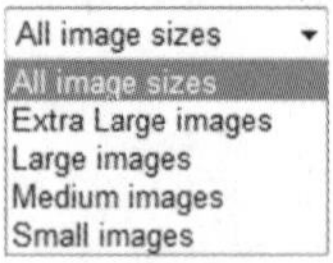

The results page, shown in Fig. 2.23 on the facing page and in colour in **G7**, opens with an array of spectacular image thumbnails (in our case anyway). You can select the size, or resolution, of images to be searched for by selecting from the **Showing** drop-down menu (Fig. 2.22).

Fig. 2.22
Drop-down
Menu

Clicking on one of the thumbnails opens another page, see Fig. 2.24, with a frame at the top showing the image and giving some background on it, with the Web page on which the image is located open below. To see a larger version of the image click the **See full-size image** link on this page. The **Image Results** link steps you back to the full results page.

Fig. 2.23 Part of a Typical Google Image Search Results Page

Fig. 2.24 Details of a Selected Image

Google analyses in its search indexes the text on the pages next to images, the captions and filenames of embedded images and other factors to make its image content selection for a search. The highest quality images are usually presented first in the results.

If the results page contains photographs 'with adult content' and that is not what you wanted, you can click the **Moderate SafeSearch is on** link to open Google's Global Preferences sheet. On this you can select options from the **SafeSearch Filtering** box shown in Fig. 2.25. The choice is yours.

Fig. 2.25 Controlling Adult Content of Search Results

The default setting is to **Use moderate filtering**. This works well with us, but with some searches the **Use strict filtering** option may be needed.

Don't forget that the photographs shown in the search results will actually belong to someone and may be protected by copyright. You should not use such material without contacting the site owner and getting permission.

Have fun looking through the enormous volume of images available, but don't forget to come back and finish this book!

3

Online Shopping

These days more and more people are using the Web for much of their shopping. After all it's quick and easy and you don't have to get the car out of the garage. This is not a bad trend, but we hope a balance is maintained so that we don't see the demise of all of our local and town centre shops.

If you want to find and buy something specific on the Web, you can do an ordinary Google Web search for the item and plough through scores of pages which may, or may not be useful, or you can use Google's shopping feature – Google Product Search.

Google Product Search

This shopping search engine helps you find the items you want, both online and in nearby stores. It isn't a store itself but a searchable database of millions of products. You can view photographs, sort results by price or store location, see reviews and select a price range. Product Search collects a wide array of options for you and provides the tools so that you can find the best buy.

Google Product Search collects product information in two ways. It uses information submitted by sellers who want to use the free service. Also, as the Google spidering software crawls the Internet, it automatically identifies Web pages that offer products for sale. The results are automatically generated and Google is adamant that they do not accept payment for inclusion of products in their search results, nor do they place sellers' sites higher in the results if they are advertisers.

Froogle

Google Product Search was originally known as Froogle (pronounced frugal), but was renamed in April 2007. The pun had proved to be too obscure for most of us, and there were copyright and trademark problems as well.

Using Google Product Search

The easiest way to open the Product Search window is to click on the **Shopping** link at the top left corner of a Google page. You can also enter the following URL into your browser's Address Bar for the UK version.

www.google.co.uk/products

Fig. 3.1 The Google Product Search Page

To begin a Google Product Search you enter a keyword such as a product name, model number or brand name, or a combination of these, into the search box shown above and click the **Search Products** button.

Sometimes if you do a Google Web search you will get a **Shopping results** section, like the one in Fig. 3.2 below.

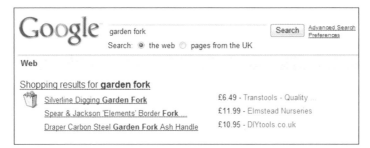

Fig. 3.2 Shopping Results from a Google Search

You can then click this link to go to Google Product Search, as we did in our example below (Fig. 3.3).

Fig. 3.3 Typical Google Product Search Results

Here we have searched for a rather mundane object to help keep our garden trim.

The search results include price, brand, a description, and usually a photograph. Near the top is a drop-down box that lets you sort the results by relevance (the default), price, seller rating or by product rating.

The results in Fig. 3.3 are shown in list view, with a single vertical column of search results including product descriptions. You can also click the **Show grid view** link to see them in a more compact page of 20 thumbnail-sized products that include fewer product details.

Sponsored Links

As mentioned previously, Google Product Search unlike many other price comparison services does not charge fees for listings, nor accept payment for products to show higher up in the results lists. Anyone can submit individual product information through Google Base. Google, however does sell advertising (through AdWords) to be displayed in Product Search results as Sponsored links, which are placed adjacent to the unpaid results.

Usually we tend to ignore the Sponsored Links on Google's results pages, but those on the Product Search pages are well worth looking at, especially if you are considering making a purchase anyway.

Refining Search Results

If you go to the bottom of a Product Search results page you will find several ways to refine the search results, as shown in Fig. 3.4 below.

Fig. 3.4 Refining Product Search Results

You can set a price range and search within it by entering your lowest possible price in the left **£** box, your highest possible price in the right box and clicking on **Go**. You can also search by different **Brands**, **Shops** and **Seller ratings**.

All in all this is a good tool, which seems to be changing quite quickly. We wouldn't be at all surprised to see it called Google Shopping before long, also the American site doesn't always work quite the same as the UK one. Perhaps because Google are experimenting more there.

Google Checkout

One problem with shopping online is that you have to pay for what you buy. This usually means that you have to re-enter the same name, address, phone number, and credit card information for every transaction you make, which can be a bore. One way to solve the problem is to use Google Checkout, an option that makes buying across the Web fast, safe and easy.

The main feature of Google Checkout is that once you are logged in to Google you can buy from stores without having to login again – no more entering the same information each time you buy, and no more having to remember different usernames and passwords for each store. Of course this only works on Web sites that are themselves registered with Google Checkout. These will have the [Google Checkout] logo icon in a prominent position on the page. This is an easy way to identify fast, secure places to shop when you search. And after you've placed your order, Google Checkout provides a purchase history where you can track your orders and shipping information in one place.

Creating a Google Account

You cannot use Google Checkout unless you have an account with Google, so if you don't have an account, go to

www.google.co.uk (see Fig. 2.1) to open the Google Accounts Sign in window shown in Fig. 3.5.

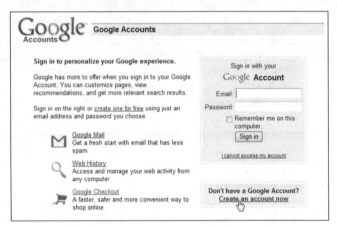

Fig. 3.5 The Google Accounts Login Window

Now click the **Create an account now** link pointed to above, fill out the required fields in the window that opens, and click **I accept. Create my account**.

To check that the e-mail address you associated with your account is correct, Google sends a message to it. So check your e-mail for this verification message from Google. Open the message and click on the link provided to activate your Google Account. That's it done, you now have a Google account.

Signing in to Google Checkout

You still have to sign in to Checkout though, and provide your personal details. To do this, either attempt to make a transaction with Google Checkout, or go to the following page, **http://checkout.google.com**, shown in Fig. 3.6 and in colour in **G8** and click **Sign up now**.

Then, as long as you are happy to do so, enter your personal information in the next window, shown in Fig. 3.7. When all the required boxes are complete click the **Create my account. Time to shop!** button.

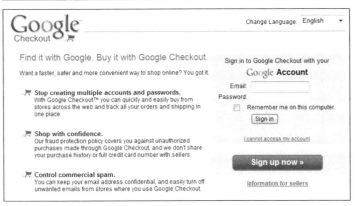

Fig. 3.6 Signing up to Google Checkout

Google
Checkout

Welcome to Google Checkout !

Sign up for a free Google Account in order to use Google Checkout : A faster, safer and more convenient way to shop online.

Your current email address:

Choose a password: Password strength:

Minimum of 8 characters in length.

Re-enter password:

Location: United States

Card number:

Expiration date: mm   / yyyy   CVC: What's this?

Cardholder name:

Billing Address:

City/Town   State   Zip [?]

Phone number:

Required for account verification.

My shipping address is: ◉ My billing address
                           ◯ A different address

I agree to the Terms of Service.

Create my account. Time to shop!

Fig. 3.7 The Personal Information Needed for Google Checkout

Using Google Checkout

Now whenever you are shopping online look for the Google Checkout badge [Google Checkout], either on Google search results, or on merchant's own Web pages. Shopping at these sites should be fast, easy and secure.

When you are ready to pay for your purchases go to the site's checkout page as usual, but click on the Google Checkout button [Google Checkout] and sign in with your Google Checkout username and password. You then confirm your delivery and payment information by clicking the **Place your order now** button. Before doing this though, you can control whether you want to receive promotional e-mails from the store.

In the future, you can track the progress of your order by going to your Google Checkout account. As before go to **http://checkout.google.com** and enter your username and password.

Your credit card will be charged for your transactions by Google, not by individual traders. Each one will have the entry "GOOGLE * TraderName" on your credit card statement. A word of warning though, if you have an American Express card you will not be able to use it with Google Checkout for a non $US transaction. An annoying weakness, we feel.

Web History

Once you have opened an account with Google, the Google Accounts window we saw on Fig. 3.5 gives you access to another feature you may be interested in – Web History.

With this you can view and search across the full text of the pages you have previously visited, including Google searches, Web pages, images, videos and news stories. If you use Web History over a long period it can help deliver more personalised search results based on your previous Web usage.

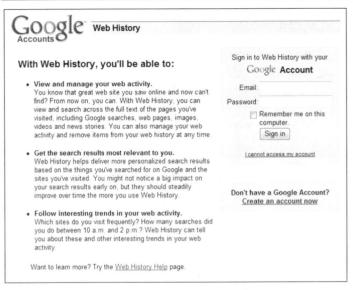

Fig. 3.8 Signing in to Google Web History

All you need to make Web History work, is a Google Account and the Google Toolbar with PageRank enabled (see the next Chapter). The Toolbar, as part of your browser, helps Google associate the pages you visit with your Google Account.

To reach your Web history, use a **Web History** link from a Google page, or go to it directly at:

www.google.com/history

If you want to find out more about Web History we suggest you click the **Web History Help** link shown at the bottom of Fig. 3.8. This opens the Help page shown in Fig. 3.9 on the next page for you to work through.

Some Reservations

Once you have Web History set up it keeps track of everywhere you go on the Web, what you search for and what you view on the Internet, as long as you're signed into your Google account. There are lots of handy uses for this.

Fig. 3.9 Getting Help on Google Web History

You can search your history to find information you remember seeing a while ago, but can't remember where. You can see what sites you visit most often, what you most often search for and even on what days and months you do most of your searching.

But there are strong privacy issues. Many people will not be happy with a tool that can monitor the Web activity of everyone that uses their computer.

If you feel that way, you can easily remove it. Log-in to your Google Account, click the **Edit** link at the top of the **My products** list, and select **Delete Web History**. Following the instructions on the next screen should permanently remove Web History from your account.

We find it a little scary that Google has so much information on us. Talk about Big Brother, and not the TV show either!

4

The Google Toolbar

One of our favourite Google tools is version 5 of the Toolbar, which places Google's capabilities on a bar at the top of your browser window. You can then use most of Google's features by typing and clicking buttons on this bar without having to open a Google home page.

Installing the Toolbar

Google Toolbar 5 is designed to run on Internet Explorer 6 or Firefox 2 (and above) browsers, running under Microsoft Windows 2000 (SP3+), Windows XP, or Windows Vista. It can also be run with Firefox on some Linux platforms. We will step through the installation on Internet Explorer, but the others are very similar. Open the Web page:

http://toolbar.google.com/t5

and click the **Install Google Toolbar 5 BETA** button shown below in Fig. 4.1.

Fig. 4.1 Installing Google Toolbar

Fig. 4.2 Installing Google Toolbar – Terms of Service

On the window that opens, shown in Fig. 4.2 above, have a good look at Google's Terms of Service, we suggest you accept the default settings in the **Configure your Toolbar** section and finally click the **Accept and Download** button.

When you see the **File Download** window, click the **Run** button and the installation will start. If you are asked, make sure you give your firewall permission to let the Toolbar functions make contact with Google. Hopefully the installation will be carried out without too many problems, although it took us two attempts the first time we tried.

When the operation is complete, a page will open (see **G9**) telling you that Google Toolbar is now installed in your browser, and you should be able to see it at the top of your Explorer browser window, as in Fig. 4.3 below.

Fig. 4.3 The Google Toolbar in Position

Toolbar Features

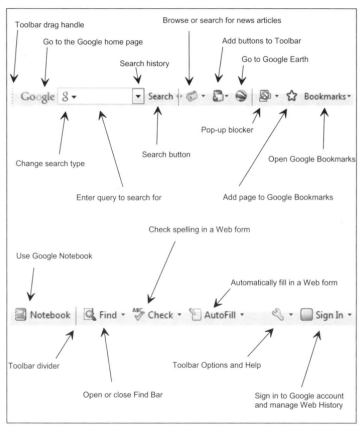

Fig. 4.4 Parts of the Default Google Toolbar

The default toolbar consists of a search query entry box, buttons you can click to perform different actions and down-arrows ▼ you click to open other features or drop-down menus.

These features are located in Fig. 4.4 above, and described in more detail in the next few pages. For display purposes the bar has been split into two sections in Fig. 4.4.

Google Home Page

 Clicking this button opens your default Google home page. Which Google page opens is controlled in the **Toolbar Options** box, shown in Fig. 4.5 below, and opened by clicking the **Toolbar Options** button 🖫. To default to Google UK, make sure the **Search**, **Use Google site** setting is as shown here.

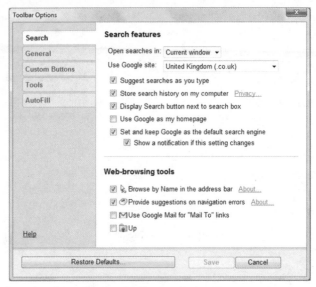

Fig. 4.5 The Toolbar Options Box

Enhanced Search Box

 This is the heart of the Toolbar and consists of several parts. If you click the 8 icon in the search box you can select which Google site will be used for the search. The default is Web search. As you would expect, you type your search query into the search box, but as you do you will see a list of suggestions based on popular Google searches, spelling corrections and your own Toolbar search history and bookmarks (Fig. 4.6). This may save you some typing, but probably not!

Clicking the down-arrow ▼ gives a similar list, but containing the search terms you have recently used.

When you are happy with the query entry in the text box, clicking the **Search** button  will start the search, which will display on the active browser sheet below. You can

Fig. 4.6 Suggestions

control the width of the entry box by dragging the slider button ⁑ to the left or right.

Custom Buttons

With support for Google Gadgets, live feeds and custom site search, the custom buttons of Google Toolbar version 5 are quite something. Try the Google News button ⊞⁃. If you click the button, Google News will open in the active browser page, but if you click the down-arrow ▼ to the right, the News gadget drops down from the Toolbar, and closes when you are done with it, as shown in Fig. 4.7 and **G10**.

Fig. 4.7 Using the News Drop-down Gadget

Clicking , the Add Buttons icon, gives a drop-down list of new buttons to add, with the **Button Gallery** option giving you access to hundreds more.

Fig. 4.8 Adding Buttons to the Toolbar

Pop-up Blocker

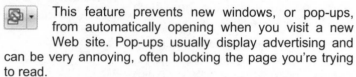 This feature prevents new windows, or pop-ups, from automatically opening when you visit a new Web site. Pop-ups usually display advertising and can be very annoying, often blocking the page you're trying to read.

By default all pop-ups are blocked. To allow them from the current Web site, just click the **Pop-up Blocker** button, which should change design from **Pop-ups blocked** to **Pop-ups allowed** . If you allow pop-ups on a Web site, this preference will be remembered for future visits.

To allow pop-ups from a link on the page press the **Ctrl** key as you click the link.

PageRank

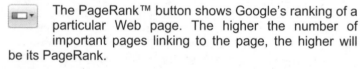 The PageRank™ button shows Google's ranking of a particular Web page. The higher the number of important pages linking to the page, the higher will be its PageRank.

This feature has to be enabled in the **Tools** tab of the **Toolbar Options** box, shown earlier in Fig. 4.5, opened by clicking the **Toolbar Options** button . Select the **PageRank** checkbox and click the **Save** button.

 Once enabled, to view a Web site's ranking, you just hover your mouse cursor over the **PageRank** button.

It is worth remembering though, that when PageRank is enabled the Google Toolbar sends information about the pages you are viewing to the Google servers. This data is stored and then used to compile your Web History. If, for privacy reasons, you don't want this to happen, you should disable PageRank by 'deselecting' the **PageRank** checkbox in the **Toolbar Options** box.

Toolbar Bookmarks

 The Bookmarks feature lets you save shortcuts to your favourite Web pages, and navigate to them in seconds, no matter where you are. Unlike your browser's bookmarks these are stored online on your Google Account, so you can access them from the Toolbar of any computer with an Internet connection.

To add a Bookmark, sign in to your Google Account, as described in the last Chapter, and click the **Bookmarks** button 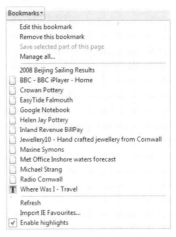. To access your bookmarks on the Toolbar, click the **Bookmarks** button Bookmarks▾, as shown in Fig. 4.9.

Once you are signed in you can import your Web browser's bookmarks, (called Favorites by Microsoft). Click the down-arrow next to the Bookmarks button and depending on your browser, select **Import IE Favorites** or **Import Firefox**

Fig. 4.9 Toolbar Bookmarks

Bookmarks. In the page that opens, select the checkboxes next to the bookmarks you want and click the **Import** button.

Notebook

 Google Notebook, included with Toolbar 5, makes clipping, collecting and sharing information as you browse the Web very easy. Once you are signed in to Google Accounts you can launch the mini-notebook window shown in Fig. 4.10, by simply clicking on the **Notebook** button. Notebooks will also appear in the Bookmarks list, and you can navigate to all saved links from the **Bookmarks** menu.

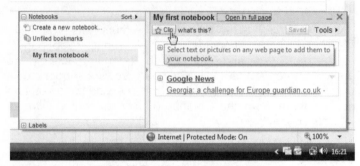

Fig. 4.10 The Mini-notebook Window

The mini-notebook window opens in the bottom-right corner of your browser window. To add clippings to your Google Notebook, highlight the text, image or link on a Web page, and click on the star button in your mini-notebook, as shown in Fig. 4.10 above and in **G11**. Another way is to just right-click on the text, image or link you want and select **Note this (Google Notebook)** from the context menu.

This can be a very useful tool, but we must admit to not using it very much. If you want to explore it further we suggest you start from the following Web page:

www.google.com/googlenotebook/faq.html

The Find Button and Find Bar

Finding a particular word on a Web page can be difficult without the Toolbar. But with it you can use the **Find** bar to search an open Web page for specific words or phrases.

Clicking the **Find** button on the Toolbar, or pressing **Ctrl+F** on the keyboard, opens the **Find** bar, as shown in Fig. 4.11, at the bottom of the browser window.

Fig. 4.11 The Find Bar

Once the **Find** bar is open you can enter a search term in the **Find** field, and as you type, you will see the results highlighted on the page. To cycle through the matching results on the page, click the **Next** and **Previous** buttons on the bar. To highlight all matching results at once, click the **Highlight all** button, which highlights each search word in a different colour. To see this, have a look at **G13** which shows a very colourful example of the procedure.

Individual words typed in the **Find** field appear as separate buttons on the **Find** bar, as shown in **G13**. To search the page for one of these individual words just click its button. To close the **Find** bar when you have finished searching you click the **Find** button on the Toolbar.

If you can't see a **Find** button on your Toolbar don't worry, you need to enable it. Just click the **Toolbar Options** button ✎, click the Tools tab in the **Toolbar Options** box, select the **Find bar** checkbox, pointed to in Fig. 4.12 and finally click the **Save** button.

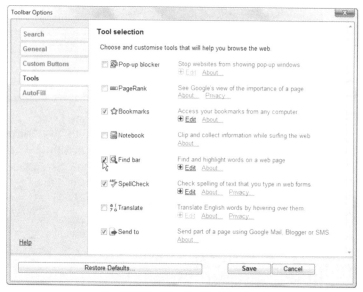

Fig. 4.12 Enabling the Find Bar Tool

SpellCheck

 Google Toolbar's new SpellCheck button finds any spelling mistakes when you type text into a Web page, such as a form, Web-based email and discussion forums.

In our example below (and in **G12**) we weren't sure we had spelt the word 'purchassing' correctly, so we clicked the **SpellCheck** button.

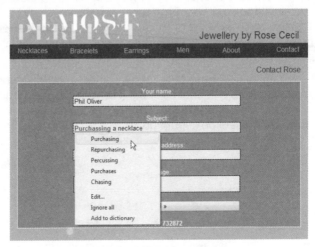

Fig. 4.13 Spell Checking a Web Form

The incorrect word was changed to underlined red, as shown, and the **SpellCheck** button changed to the **Stop** button . Clicking the incorrect word produced a drop-down list of suggestions. We selected the first option and the word was corrected and changed to green.

To choose your SpellCheck language, click the button's down-arrow, and select a language from the **Choose language** menu, shown here.

Fig. 4.14 SpellCheck Language Options

If you choose **Auto** from this menu SpellCheck will automatically detect any of the languages listed.

To automatically correct all spelling mistakes on a Web form, click the down-arrow next to the SpellCheck button, and choose the **AutoFix** option.

Translate

 If you work at all with foreign languages this button will be of help to you. It has two basic functions. You can use the **Word Translator** feature to translate English words on a Web page into another language, or select **Translate this page** from the Toolbar's drop-down menu to view French, German, Italian, Portuguese, Spanish, Simplified Chinese, Japanese, and Korean Web pages in English.

The Translate button will not be on your Toolbar by default, so you may need to enable it. Just click the **Toolbar Options** button 🖉, click the Tools tab in the **Toolbar Options** box, select the **Translate** checkbox, shown in Fig. 4.15 below.

Fig. 4.15 Enabling the Translate Tool and Choosing Language

If you want to see word translations in Spanish, that is the default, so just click the **Save** button. To work with other languages, click the **Edit** button next to the **Translate** checkbox, and select a language from the drop-down menu shown in Fig. 4.15. Clicking the **Close** button followed by the **Save** button will activate the change.

To use the Word Translator click the **Translate** button  on the Toolbar and then hover your mouse cursor over an English word on a Web page to view its translation.

Fig. 4.16 Translating Words from English to French

Word Translator supports translation from English into French, German, Italian, Spanish, Traditional and Simplified Chinese, Japanese, Russian, and Korean.

Many International sites provide different language versions of their Web pages, but many don't. All may not be lost though if you are struggling with a foreign page and have the Google Toolbar. Just click the down-arrow next to the **Translate** button and select the **Translate Page into English** option, as shown here. These days automatic translation is getting very good!

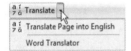

Fig. 4.17 Web Page Translation

AutoFill

 It seems the more we get involved with life on the Internet, the more times we have to type the same information into forms on Web pages. We saw earlier that Google Checkout is one way to ease this load, yet another is the **AutoFill** feature on the Toolbar. Once you have it set up, this lets you to fill out details of your name, address and e-mail on Web forms with a single click. Unfortunately phone number entry is set for US numbers and we did not find it so easy!

Before setting up AutoFill make sure you sign in to your Google Account, as described in the last Chapter. If you don't do this, the AutoFill details will only be available on your own computer. Then to set up AutoFill, click the **Toolbar Options** button , and click the AutoFill tab in the **Toolbar Options** box to open the AutoFill settings sheet.

Colour Gallery 1

G1 A Special Logo for Google's 10th Birthday Celebrations

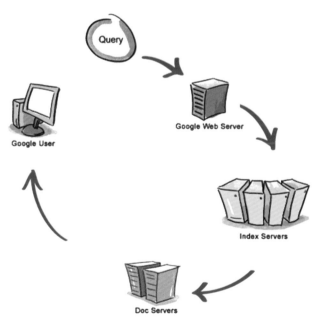

G2 The Life of a Google Query

Web   Images   News   Maps   Products   Groups   **more »**

[Search the Web]

More Google products

Search

 Alerts
Receive news and search results via email

 Blog Search
Find blogs on your favorite topics

 Book Search
Search the full text of books

 Checkout
Complete online purchases more quickly and securely

 Google Chrome^{New!}
A browser built for speed, stability and security

 Desktop
Search your own computer

 Directory
Browse the web by topic

 Earth
Explore the world from your PC

 Finance
Business info, news, and interactive charts

 Product Search
Search for stuff to buy

 Images
Search for images on the web

 Maps
View maps and directions

 News
Search thousands of news stories

 Notebook^{New!}
Clip and collect information as you surf the web

 Scholar
Search scholarly papers

 Special Searches
Search within specific topics

 Toolbar
Add a search box to your browser

 University Search
Search a specific university's website

 Video
Search videos and upload your own

 Web Search
Search over 8 billion web pages

 Web Search Features
Do more with search

Explore and innovate

 Code
Download APIs and open source code

 Labs
Try out new Google products

Communicate, show & share

 Blogger
Express yourself online

 Calendar
Organise your schedule and share events with friends

 Docs
Create and share your online documents, presentations, and spreadsheets

Google Mail
Fast, searchable email with less spam

Groups
Create mailing lists and discussion groups

orkut **Orkut**
Meet new people and stay in touch with friends

 Picasa
Find, edit and share your photos

 Talk
IM and call your friends through your computer

 Translate
View web pages in other languages

You **YouTube**^{New!}
Watch, upload and share videos

Go mobile

 Mobile
Use Google on your mobile phone

Make your computer work better

 Pack
A free collection of essential software

G3 Google Products Available for Use in the UK. These are Accessed from a Google Home Page by Clicking the **more**, **even more** Links

G4 The Google UK Home Page in the Google Chrome Browser

G5 An Instant Local Weather Forecast

G6 A Google Web Search for a Quick Map

G7 Searching with Google Images

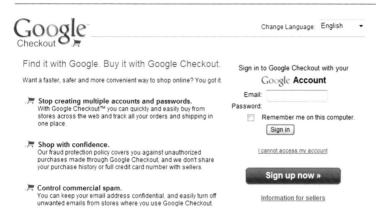

G8 Signing up to Google Checkout

G9 The Google Toolbar 5 when First Installed

G10 Using the News Drop-down Gadget on the Toolbar

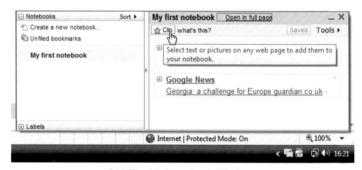

G11 The Mini-notebook Window

G12 Spell Checking a Web Form from the Toolbar

Home | The Artist | Statement | Tate Gallery 1 | Tate Gallery 2

MICHAEL STRANG AT TATE ST IVES

Purchase the Book Online

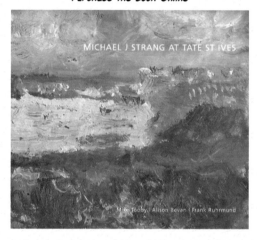

In 1995 a series of Michael Strang's studies were included in the "Century of Images" exhibition held at the Tate Gallery, St Ives. These small rapid studies in oil were painted that year, *en plein aire* at and around Porthmeor Beach, near the Tate Gallery.

50 of them have now been included in the new book:

MICHAEL J STRANG AT TATE ST IVES

Forward by Alison Bevan, Director of Penlee House Gallery & Museum, Penzance
A statement by Mike Tooby, then the Curator of Tate St Ives
An Introduction by Frank Ruhrmund, Western Morning News, West Briton and Cornishman newspapers.

G13 Using the Toolbar Find Button and Find Bar
to Search for Words on a Web Page

AutoFill settings

☑ 📄 AutoFill - fill web forms (name, address, etc.) with a single click   About...

Select the default item with which to fill web forms.

Profiles   Add new profile

⊙ Set as default profile   ⊟ Close

          Label: PRMO Sample
              e.g. work info

Name and email

    First name: Phil

  Middle name: Robin Martin

    Last name: Oliver

        Email: prmo@sample.com

Company name: Personal

Address

Postal address

      Address: The Cottage

             Stringy Lane

  City/Town: Truro

     County: Cornwall

   Postcode: TR1 6UA

    Country: England

      ☑ Billing address is same as postal

Contact numbers

	country code	area code	number
Phone:			
Fax:			

⊟ Close

Credit cards   Add new credit card

You currently have no credit cards stored. Add new credit card

☐ Require password to access credit card information

G14 A New AutoFill Profile Sheet with Fictional Data

G15 A Search in the Google Toolbar Button Gallery

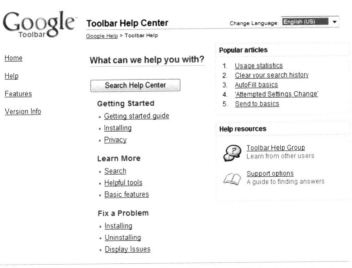

G16 The Google Toolbar Help Center

Web Images Maps **News** Shopping Mail more ▼   Sign in

Google News™

[Search News] [Search the Web]

Search and browse 4,500 news sources updated continuously.

Standard Version | Text Version | Image Version   News archive search | Advanced news search | Blog search

Top Stories U.S.   ▼   [Go]   Auto-generated 28 Aug at 11:21 GMT

+363
Day 3 of the don...
Kansas City Star

+273
EU considers san...
BBC News

+110
Gustav nears Ja...
The Associated Press

Same-sex marriage ban is losing, state pollsters say
Ventura County Star - 3 hours ago

+24
Miliband warns...
BBC News

+4
Same-sex marria...
Ventura County Star

+16
Ted Stevens win...
Seattle Times

Ted Stevens wins Alaska primary; House race undecided
Seattle Times - 4 hours ago

Lesbian pioneer Del Martin dies
Bay Area Reporter - 6 hours ago

Fannie Shuffles Its Top Leaders
Washington Post - 7 hours ago

+17
Lesbian pioneer...
Bay Area Reporter

+6
Fannie Shuffles...
Washington Post

71 related images
Hurricane fears r...
BBC News

Hurricane fears raise oil prices
BBC News - 2 hours ago
Oil prices have risen for a fourth straight day on fears that Tropical Storm Gustav may disrupt US production in the Gulf of Mexico. With Gustav now heading towards Jamaica after battering Haiti on Wednesday, US light crude was up 93 cents to $119.08 a ...
71 related images »

G17 Part of a Google News Page in Image Version

News results: Standard Version | Text Version | **Image Version** Results 1 - 25 of about **111** related articles. Search took **0.06**

Sort by relevance   Sorted by date   Sort by date with duplicates included

Hurricane Gusta...
E Canada Now

Haiti hurricane
Portugal Resident

Gustav may bec...
CTV.ca

Hurricane Gustav Death Toll Increases To Over 20
E Canada Now - 39 minutes ago
Washington (ECN) - The death toll from Hurricane Gustav continues to rise, as 22 people have been confirmed to have died as of Wednesday night from the ...

Gustav Nears Ja...
ABC News

Gustav nears Ja...
The Associated Press

Gustav Nears Ja...
News Channel 7

Haiti hurricane
Portugal Resident - 50 minutes ago

Gustav may become hurricane today: forecasters
CTV.ca - 1 hour ago

Gustav Nears Jamaica as New Orleans Keeps Watch
ABC News - 1 hour ago

Huntsville's Wee...
About - Cities &

Gustav kills 22 in...
AFP

America gets rea...
CBBC Newsround

Gustav nears Jamaica as New Orleans keeps watch
The Associated Press - 2 hours ago

Gustav Nears Jamaica; New Orleans Keeps Watch
News Channel 7 - 3 hours ago

G18 Some of the '71 related images' Pointed to in G17

Web Images Maps News Shopping Mail more ▼

Google UK
Finance BETA

e.g. "VOD" or "Barclays"

[Get quotes]

Market summary

11:22AM BST

Virgin leads airline plot to buy Gatwick
Times Online -
41 minutes ago

Virgin Atlantic has held talks with financial partners over a possible bid to buy Gatwick Airport .....

Sky News

Virgin eyes up Gatwick in potential £2bn deal CityWire co.uk

Branson lays out airline plan for Gatwick This is Money

BBC News

Related articles »

FTSE 100	5,616.10	+13.30	(0.24%)
FTSE 250	9,562.80	+153.30	(1.63%)
FTSE All Share	2,866.12	+11.00	(0.39%)
techMARK 100	1,636.56	+14.62	(0.90%)
GBP-USD	1.8017	-0.0186	(-1.02%)
GBP-Euro	1.2338	-0.0082	(-0.66%)
GBP-Yen	194.8360	-3.3742	(-1.70%)

— FTSE 100 — FTSE 250
— FTSE All Share — techMARK 100

+2.01%
+1.01%
0.00%
-1.01%

10am   12pm   2pm   4pm

Top stories | Market | Recent quote related

Hays warns of weak UK jobs market
BBC News - 31 minutes ago

Recruitment consultancy Hays has posted a 25% increase in annual profits after a sharp rise .....

Recruiter Hays to cut jobs Reuters UK
Related articles »

Brown announces stamp duty holiday in housing rescue package
Times Online - 37 minutes ago

Properties costing less than £175000 will be exempt from stamp duty for the next year .....

Brown Suspends UK Stamp Duty in Moves to Spur Housing Market
Bloomberg
Related articles »

UK recession this year, OECD says
BBC News - Related articles »

Struggling sterling hits new lows
BBC News - Related articles »

Belhaven beats 'challenging' market conditions with a strong sales ...
Scotsman - Related articles »

Rebrand spells the Absolute end for Virgin Radio name
Scotsman - Related articles »

Telecoms: Former BT boss picks up the pieces at Alcatel-Lucent
guardian.co.uk - Related articles »

Construction falls for sixth consecutive month
Times Online - Related articles »

View all of today's news »

Recent quotes

Name	Price	Change	MktCap
VOD	144.10	+3.65 (2.60%)	76,290.79M
RBS	243.00	+7.25 (3.08%)	39,226.23M
HSBA	889.00	+20.25 (2.33%)	106,890.63M
BARC	366.75	+13.00 (3.67%)	29,869.38M
LLOY	313.00	+5.50 (1.79%)	18,040.18M
TSCO	394.70	+5.90 (1.52%)	31,001.06M
BAY	277.25	+15.50 (5.92%)	3,197.01M
BP	510.50	-10.50 (-2.02%)	95,716.66M

Sector summary

Sector	Change	% down/up
Basic Materials	-3.28%	
Capital Goods	+1.06%	
Conglomerates	+1.82%	
Cons. Cyclical	+2.57%	
Cons. Non-Cyclical	+1.29%	
Energy	-2.40%	
Financial	+2.02%	
Healthcare	+1.03%	
Services	+2.16%	
Technology	+1.67%	
Transportation	+3.23%	
Utilities	+0.05%	

Trends | Price | Mkt Cap | Vol

Gainers	Change	Mkt Cap
Wm. Morrison Supermarkets...	16.41%	3,028.88M
Persimmon plc	9.28%	1,263.31M
easyJet plc	8.83%	1,570.57M
Mitchells & Butlers plc	7.65%	1,222.43M
Inchcape plc	7.12%	1,264.66M

Losers	Change	Mkt Cap
Wellstream Holdings PLC	-7.15%	1,280.87M
Venture Production Plc	-6.90%	1,091.61M
Dana Petroleum plc	-6.84%	1,166.08M
Tullow Oil plc	-5.31%	5,428.51M
Aquarius Platinum Limited...	-5.01%	1,179.89M

Excludes stocks with mkt cap less than £1,000M See FAQ

International Google Finance: U.S. - Canada - 中国版 (China)

G19 Google Finance UK Home Page

Find more results for RR

News | Blogs | Feeds

Newer news | Latest news

A Avingtrans enters into Long Term Agreement with Rolls-Royce Group -...
RTT News - Sep 2, 2008

B Innovest Confirms Rolls-Royce Group's IVA Rating
CSRwire.com (press release) - Aug 28, 2008

C Goodrich and Rolls-Royce Propose Engine Controls Joint Venture
Carolina Newswire (press release) - Aug 15, 2008

D Rolls-Royce, Goodrich to Form Engine-Controls Venture (Update1)
Bloomberg - Aug 14, 2008
UPDATE 1-Rolls Royce, Goodrich propose engine controls JV Hemscott
Rolls-Royce, Goodrich to Form Joint Venture for

Older news | View all news for RR » | Subscribe

Related Companies

Name	Exchange	Symbol	Last Trade		Change	Mkt Cap
Rolls-Royce Group plc (ADR)	OTC	RYCEY	36.30*	-0.25	(-0.68%)	13,301.31M
Goodrich Corporation	NYSE	GR	51.42	+0.17	(0.33%)	6,432.90M
Honeywell International Inc.	NYSE	HON	50.20	+0.03	(0.06%)	37,370.71M
Meggitt plc	LON	MGGT	236.50*	-4.75	(-1.97%)	1,576.99M
Hampson Industries PLC	LON	HAMP	182.50*	-1.25	(-0.68%)	289.47M
HEICO Corporation	NYSE	HEI	34.73	-0.90	(-2.53%)	916.05M
Senior plc	LON	SNR	112.25*	+0.25	(0.22%)	444.24M

Key Stats & Ratios

	Quarterly (Jun '08)	Annual (2007)	Annual (TTM)
Net Profit Margin	7.21%	8.07%	7.46%
Operating Margin	7.93%	6.91%	8.03%
EBITD Margin	-	9.16%	10.52%
Return on Average Assets	4.92%	5.39%	5.12%
Return on Average Equity	16.08%	19.38%	16.88%
Employees	38,500	-	-

More Resources

Analyst Estimates - BusinessWeek
Options - MarketWatch
Research Reports - Reuters
Director Dealings - Yahoo Finance

Discussions

Rolls Royce Share Price

Events

Jul 24, 2008   Interim 2008 Earnings Conference Call (Fixed Income)

Summary

Rolls-Royce Group plc is a global business providing power systems for use on land, at sea and in the air. It operates in four segments: Civil aerospace, which is engaged in the development, manufacture, marketing and sales of commercial aero engines and aftermarket services; Defense aerospace, which is engaged in the development, manufacture, marketing and sales of military aero engines and aftermarket services; Marine, which is engaged in the development, manufacture, marketing and sales of marine propulsion systems and aftermarket services, and Energy, which is engaged in the development, manufacture, marketing and sales of power systems for the offshore oil and gas industry, electrical power generation and aftermarket services. In October 2007, the Company announced the acquisition of Seaworthy Systems Inc., a United States-based naval architecture and engineering firm.

65 Buckingham Gate
London, ENG SW1E 6AT
United Kingdom - Map
+44-20-72229020 (Phone)
+44-20-72279178 (Fax)

Company website:
http://www.rolls-royce.com/
News Releases,
Investor Relations,
Financial Information,
Corporate History/Profile,
Executives, Products/Services,
Employment Opportunities

Officers and directors

John E. Rose »	Chief Executive Officer and Director
James M. Guyette »	Officer Since: 1996 Age: 55 America, Inc. Director

G20 A Google Finance Get Quotes Page
with Share Price and Company Information

G21 A Google Mail Inbox List of Messages in Colour

G22 An Automatic Stacking of a Conversation showing the Originator,
and Subsequent Participants in Different Colours

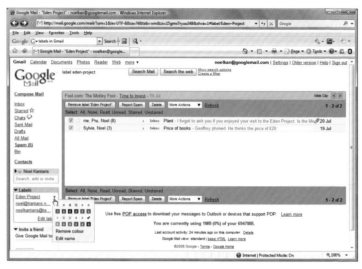

G23 Assigning Colours to Labelled E-mail Messages

G24

G25

G26

G27

G28

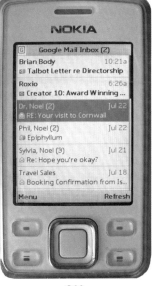

G29

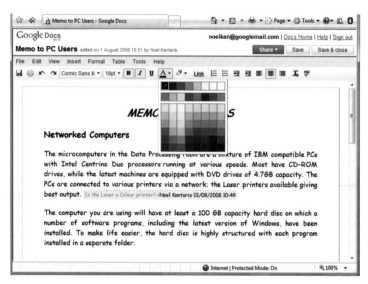

G30 Assigning Colours to Document Comments

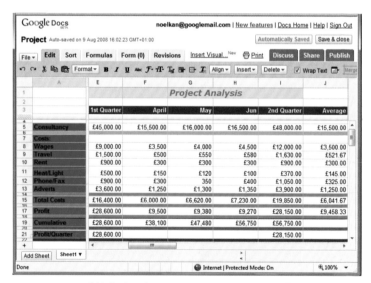

G31 Project Analysis of ADEPT Consultants

Fig. 4.18 Enabling AutoFill Settings

Make sure the **AutoFill** checkbox is selected as in Fig. 4.18 above, and click on the **Add new profile** link pointed to. This opens a **Profile** section to the sheet as we show completed with fictional data in **G14**.

Now you just enter your personal information into the fields. Don't forget that, unless you signed in, the information you store in AutoFill can be viewed by whoever else uses your computer. There is the facility to save a password protected credit card number, but we think this is probably not a good idea in these days of identity theft. When you have finished click the **Close** link.

When you next click the **AutoFill** button down-arrow you should see the new Profile in the drop-down menu, as shown in Fig. 4.19. If you have multiple profiles, this lets you choose which one to use.

Fig. 4.19

As long as your Toolbar is active, the next time you visit a Web site with a blank form to fill in, just hover the mouse pointer over the **AutoFill** button and Autofill will highlight in yellow the form fields it can fill in and show the text it will use. When you click the **AutoFill** button your information will be entered. You then just have to edit or complete the entries as required.

Toolbar Options

 As we have seen several times so far, clicking the **Toolbar Options** button opens the Toolbar Options box which gives you control over how your Toolbar looks and operates. The sections looked at so far are **Search** (Fig. 4.5), **Tools** (Fig. 4.12) and **AutoFill** (Fig. 4.12).

Fig. 4.20 The General Toolbar Options

The **General** options, shown in Fig. 4.20 above, let you set the Toolbar language, whether you want text labels by the buttons, and whether you want to send usage statistics back to Google.

The **Custom Buttons** options are shown in Fig. 4.21 on the facing page. It is in this tabbed sheet that you control which buttons populate your Toolbar, and their order.

You select a button for the Toolbar by clicking in the checkbox to the left of its name, ☑ **W** Wikipedia for instance. You remove it from the Toolbar by unselecting the checkbox. You can also **Edit** buttons, but that is outside the scope of this book. If you click the **Add more buttons** link you can select from hundreds more buttons in the Google Toolbar Button Gallery, shown in colour in **G15**.

To move a button, just select it in the list and drag it up or down to where you want it.

Custom buttons and search types

Select which buttons appear in the toolbar. Drag and drop to re-order. Add more buttons..

☑ **W** Wikipedia - Wikipedia, the free encyclopedia	⊞ Edit	Remove
☐ Dictionary (Google) - Look up a definition	⊞ Edit	Remove
☐ I'm Feeling Lucky - Search and navigate to the best result	⊞ Edit	
☐ Search Site - Search only on the current website	⊞ Edit	
☐ UK - Find pages in a country	⊞ Edit	
☐ Google Images - Search the web for images	⊞ Edit	
☐ Google Video - Browse or search for video	⊞ Edit	
☑ Google News - Browse or search for news articles	⊞ Edit	
☐ Google Maps - Search within an area or neighbourhood	⊞ Edit	
☐ Google Groups - Browse or search within Google Groups di...	⊞ Edit	
☐ Google Product Search - Find products for sale	⊞ Edit	
☐ Web History - Search your Google Web History	⊞ Edit	
☐ Google Blog Search - Find blogs on your favourite topics	⊞ Edit	
☐ Google Books - Search Google Books	⊞ Edit	
☐ Google Calendar - Search Google Calendar	⊞ Edit	
☐ Google Docs - Search my Google Documents	⊞ Edit	
☐ Google Finance - Search Google Finance	⊞ Edit	
☐ Google Photos - Search Google Photos	⊞ Edit	
☐ Google Scholar - Search Google Scholar	⊞ Edit	
☑ Button Gallery - Add buttons to your Toolbar!	⊞ Edit	
☐ Google Earth	⊞ Edit	Remove

Sidebar menu:
- Search
- General
- **Custom Buttons**
- Tools
- AutoFill
- Help

Fig. 4.21 Adding and Removing Custom Buttons from the Toolbar

Clicking the **Toolbar Options** down-arrow opens the drop-down menu shown in Fig. 4.22, which includes the usual 'Help type' options. **Privacy Information** is worth looking at to find out what information Google uploads from you, and what it says it does with it.

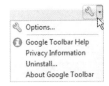

Options...
Google Toolbar Help
Privacy Information
Uninstall...
About Google Toolbar

Fig. 4.22

If you need more help with the Toolbar the **Google Toolbar Help** option is available. This opens the page shown in **G16**, and relies heavily on you knowing what Help you want to search for. This is Google after all! If after all this you are not impressed with the Google Toolbar you can click on **Uninstall** to do just that. You do have a chance to change your mind though.

Google Account Sign-in

 With version 5 of the Toolbar you can sign in to your Google account by clicking the **Sign In** button and entering your e-mail and password details. This button is grey to start with, but changes to green once you have signed in.

The Toolbar has a synchronisation feature that saves your preferences, custom buttons and AutoFill profile to your Google account. They are then available each time you sign in to the Toolbar with your Google Account. To disable this and limit your Toolbar settings to the one computer you are

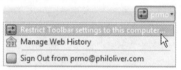

Fig. 4.23 Disabling
Synchronisation

using click the green **Sign In** button and select **Restrict Toolbar settings to this computer**. In the dialogue box that opens, click **Yes, limit settings to this computer**.

The **Manage Web History** option gives another way to control the Google Web History feature described on page 34. It opens the same window shown earlier in Fig. 3.8, but still makes you sign in again. Don't forget that you can delete items from your Web History and pause collection of Web History when you want to.

The **Sign Out from...** option should be self explanatory!

Browsing by Name

Another thing the Toolbar lets you do is to access many Web pages by name, instead of by URL. A URL is the page address that you type into your browser's address bar. This can be very useful to browse by name for Web pages that don't have obvious URLs. As an example, Camborne School of Mines is part of the Exeter University Web site but has the ridiculous URL:

www.ex.ac.uk/cornwall/academic_departments/csm/

How could anyone remember that? No problem when you have Toolbar 5, you can type **camborne school of mines** into Explorer's address bar and press **Enter** to go directly to CSM's home page.

To make sure this feature is enabled, click the **Toolbar Options** button 🖉, and click the Search tab in the **Toolbar Options** box to open the **Search** settings sheet. Select the **Browse by Name in the address bar** checkbox, as shown earlier in Fig. 4.5 and click the **Save** button.

Some Keyboard Shortcuts

To round off this chapter we include some useful keyboard shortcuts you can use with the search box of the Google Toolbar.

To go straight to the Toolbar search box without using the mouse, use the **Alt+G** keyboard combination (easy to remember as G is for Google).

I'm Feeling Lucky. Type your query in the Toolbar search box and press **Alt+Enter** to bypass the search results page and to go directly to the top result.

To open the search results in a new window, type your query and press **Shift+Enter**. You can combine this with the previous shortcut, **Alt+Shift+Enter** will open the top result in a new window. Depending on your settings, the page could open in a new tab instead of a new window.

5

Google News

These days every newspaper and other news source has a Web site showing a continuously updated online version of its news and story contents. We all like to know what is happening and where, and if you are like us, some of these sites may be the first ones you visit whenever you switch your computer on.

Google goes one step further, it 'crawls' these news sites continuously, indexes their contents and presents a summary of the news as it happens in over 40 regional editions of Google News, including News UK shown below.

Fig. 5.1 The Top Stories Section of a Google News UK Page

To access Google News just click on the **News** link at the top of a Google page, or visit **http://news.google.com** for the US version, or **www.google.co.uk/news** for the UK version. Some features are somewhat different between these versions, but the same news is available from both.

Google News Layout

Fig. 5.2 Standard Google News Page Layout

The standard, or default, Google News page consists of the Top Stories section and eight standard sections, as shown in Fig. 5.2.

These are: World, Nation (UK in our case), Business, Sci/Tech, Sport, Entertainment, Health and More Top Stories. These sections are available in all regional editions of Google News and are customisable.

The Top Stories section shows the most active stories throughout all sites, while the More Top Stories section shows the most popular stories in the Google News edition actually being viewed.

About Google News

Google News is 'untouched by human hands' as the stories, headlines and photos you see on it are selected entirely by computer algorithms, based on factors like how often and where a story appears online. The grouping and ranking of stories depends on such things as titles, text, and publication time.

The standard Google News pages include news items published in the last 30 days, but Google doesn't throw the indexed data away then. It is included in the Google News Archive looked at later in the chapter.

News Clusters

Google groups News articles about the same story together, as shown here, and calls these groups, clusters. This makes it easy to read versions of the same news from different sources, or see how a story evolves over time. Clicking on the

U.K. »   edit ☒

EU threatens sanctions against Russia
guardian.co.uk - **40 minutes ago**
David Miliband listens during a meeting with students at the National University Kyiv-Mohyla Academy, in Kiev. Photograph: Genia Savilov/AFP/Getty Images
European Union leaders will discuss sanctions against Russia ahead of an emergency summit meeting. ...
The West pledges its support for Ukraine - up to a point
Independent
Miliband warns over Russia crisis BBC News
Telegraph.co.uk - Reuters UK - International Herald Tribune - The Press Association
all 841 news articles »

Fig. 5.3 A Typical News Cluster

link to see **all 841 news articles** (in our example) about a story will open a listing of the whole cluster.

How fresh a news story is, is shown by how long ago it was posted, e.g., **40 minutes ago** for the one in Fig. 5.3 above. You click on the title to display the article.

Image or Text Version?

You can view one of three versions of Google News. A **Text** version with no photographs, the default **Standard** version with a few relevant photographs, or an **Image** version that lets you view and explore the top headlines of the day through photos instead of just text. The latter is not available on News UK, so you have to go to the US version at **http://news.google.com**. But it is well worth the effort.

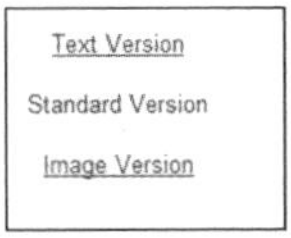

Text Version
Standard Version
Image Version

You can easily switch between these views by clicking the links shown here, located either at the top of a News page, or on the left below the section menu boxes.

To see part of a page in image view and in colour have a look at **G17**. When you move the mouse pointer over an image on the page, the full news 'snippet' is opened up on the right side of the page.

Clicking a green '**related images**' link at the bottom of an image opens images for all the stories listed, as shown in **G18**. Clicking on one of these images takes you directly to the article the image came from. You can also search for image search results by entering a search string in the **Search Box**.

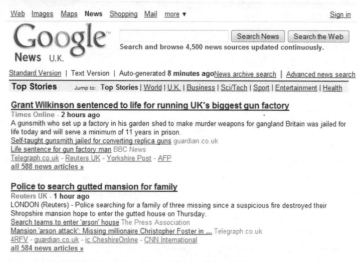

Fig. 5.4 Part of a Google News Page in Text Version

Which version you use is up to you. Even if you prefer the more standard text version with headlines, as shown in Fig. 5.4 above, viewing News with Images can be very useful. Try an Image version search for your favourite sports team, fashion model, celebrity or actress. The results can be pretty startling.

Searching Google News

You search Google News by entering your query and clicking on the **Search News** or **Search** button, depending on which page you are on.

Fig. 5.5 Searching Google News UK

By default, results are **Sorted by relevance** to your search terms as shown above. To see articles ordered chronologically you click on the **Sort by date** link at the top of the results window. You can also use the links on the left of the window to get news results from a particular day or period.

Where possible, Google adds videos to its news listings, as shown here. When there is a video available the ⊞**Video** prefix is added to the article title. Just clicking this video link opens the YouTube video player directly on the page so you can watch the video, as in Fig. 5.6 on the next page. Clicking the link again closes the video. Maybe we can see now why Google bought YouTube a few years ago.

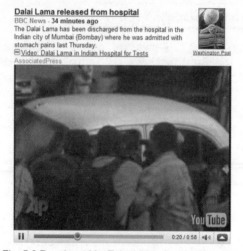

Dalai Lama released from hospital
BBC News - 34 minutes ago
The Dalai Lama has been discharged from the hospital in the Indian city of Mumbai (Bombay) where he was admitted with stomach pains last Thursday.
▣ Video: Dalai Lama in Indian Hospital for Tests
AssociatedPress

Fig. 5.6 Running a YouTube Video from a News Page

If necessary you can click the **Advanced news search** link on the News page, to confine your search to a specific news source, location, date range, or other criteria.

To limit a search to a specific country you can also specify a location for your search by entering your search terms into the search box followed by the controlling operator **location:country**. A search for **dolphins location:uk**, for example, would produce the latest news on dolphins in the UK.

You can also specify a domain in the search box using the **site:** operator followed by a domain. If you are a soccer fan the search **football site:uk** gives all the latest news. In fact this type of news search term is good for using on personalised news pages as discussed next.

Your Customised News Page

You can customise Google News (or personalize it on the US pages) so that you only see the type of news that interests you. To do this you must make sure that your browser is up to date and that it has JavaScript turned on.

The easiest way to manage a customised News page is by signing in to your Google Account. You can then access your news page from any computer anywhere, as long as it is logged onto the Internet. You can still do it without signing in but you will then be restricted to one computer and your settings will be lost whenever its cookies are cleared.

Fig. 5.7 Customising a News Page

To customise your news page, click the **Customise this page** link located near the top of the News UK home page (see Fig. 5.1). This opens the box shown here.

In this box you can move the sections you most like to read to the top of your page by dragging their icons. You can remove the sections you don't want by right-clicking them and selecting the **Delete section** option.

If you are interested in a particular topic, you can **Add a custom section** and type your search keywords (such as **football site:uk**) in the custom box. You could then automatically keep track of your favourite sport, or whatever else interests you.

Searching News Archives

Google's News Archive Search gives an easy way to search and explore historical archives, such as major newspapers, magazines, news archives and legal archives. Remember that Google stores any news over 30 days old in its News Archives database.

You can search for events, people, things, or ideas and see how they have been described over time. Search results include content that is freely accessible to everyone and that which requires a fee to access. With the latter you can usually access an overview at least, and sometimes one viewing for free.

To use this feature, you can click the **News archive search** link from the Google News home page, or go to the News Archive Search page at:

http://news.google.com/archivesearch/

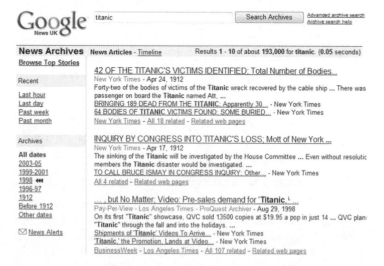

Fig. 5.8 Doing a News Archive Search for 'Titanic'

An initial archives search will show articles from **All dates** ranked according to relevance, as shown in Fig. 5.8.

You can use the date links on the left of the page to view articles for that period, or click the **Timeline** link to get a historical overview of the results by browsing an automatically created timeline.

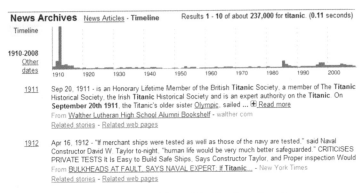

Fig. 5.9 A Timeline View of the Previous Search

The timeline, as shown above, shows graphically how the search results are grouped in time. Moving the pointer over a blue bar will show its date contents, and clicking one will open another more detailed timeline for the selected period, as shown in Fig. 5.10 below.

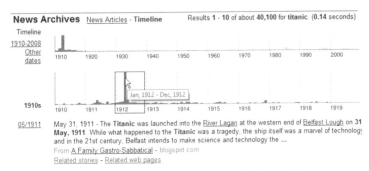

Fig. 5.10 Using a Timeline to Fine Tune Archive Search Results

News for Mobiles

Fig. 5.11 Mobile News

If you can access the Web on your mobile, you can access Google News with it, by entering the address **mobile.google.co.uk** into your phone's browser.

Google News for mobile displays sources that are designed specifically for mobile Web browsers. You can access the day's top headlines, browse news in many categories, and find the story you are looking for on the go.

To see how it would look on your phone, look at Fig. 5.11. This shows the News page for the day this was written exactly as it should appear on your mobile phone.

To see this demo and to learn more about using Google News for mobile devices go to:

http://www.google.com/mobile/default/news

If you are using an iPhone or iPod Touch you are in luck, Google News is also available formatted specially for you. It includes the complete index of news sources you would find using a desktop computer.

To access Google News on your iPhone go to **www.google.com**, click on the **more** tab and follow the link to Google News. According to Google it has received 50 times more searches from the iPhone than from any other mobile handset. This may change with their Android system!

6

Google Finance

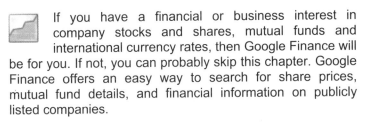 If you have a financial or business interest in company stocks and shares, mutual funds and international currency rates, then Google Finance will be for you. If not, you can probably skip this chapter. Google Finance offers an easy way to search for share prices, mutual fund details, and financial information on publicly listed companies.

It has a clean, simple interface that is easy to navigate with relevant information right on the page in front of you. Historical price information is shown in very clever interactive graphs or charts, and it has links to a wealth of relevant additional information such as, recent news stories, comparable companies and company management details.

At the time of writing there were four versions of Google Finance, US, UK, Canada and China. The UK version we look at here has been active since January 2008 so has had ample time to 'settle down'. It displays European company information, 20 minute delay actual and historical daily prices for LSE stocks back to 1996, other stock market and mutual fund data and GB£ currency quotes on its home page, as we show in **G19** in Colour Gallery 1.

Accessing Google Finance

To open Google Finance UK, either click the **Finance** link from the **more** drop-down menu on the top of a Google UK page, as shown here, or go straight to the home page at **http://finance.google.co.uk**.

Finance UK Home Page

The opening page should look something like **G19**, but obviously with different content. The main components of this page are:

Header Bar

The top section of the page shown in Fig. 6.1 below, consists of the usual Google menu along the top, with a **Get quotes** query entry box and button.

Fig. 6.1 The Google Finance UK Header Bar

You use this to search for prices of stock market companies, or mutual funds, using either their names or their ticker symbols. Google have been very clever here with their Autosuggest feature. As you type in the first part of a name a list instantly appears which suggests what you might be looking for. You just click the option

Fig. 6.2 Autosuggestion at Work

you want in the list, the ticker symbol is automatically placed in the **Get quotes** box, and the home page changes to a detailed page of data on the security you searched for. An example of which is shown in colour in **G20**.

Market Summary

This gives an overview of the current UK financial situation, with access to the main news story on the left, summarises the main current FTSE indices, and shows the main currency exchange rates.

Fig. 6.3 Market Summary Information

Clicking any of the index or currency conversion links gives you detailed current and historical data on it. Clicking the Market Chart on the right opens an interactive chart comparing the performance of the four FTSE indices over time, as in Fig. 6.4.

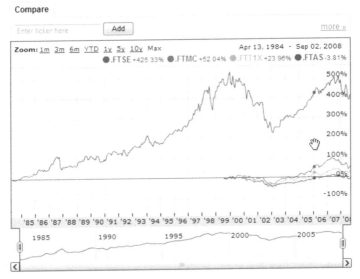

Fig. 6.4 The FTSE Indices Since 1984

Like all Google Finance charts, you can change the Zoom level on this chart, or drag the contents to see a different period.

News

News stories on Google Finance are presented by the Google News service seen in the previous chapter. The home page shows the **Top stories** for the **Market** generally, news for **Portfolio related** shares if you have a portfolio of shares open, or **Recent quote related news** if you don't. You click on tabs to move between these options.

Recent Quotes

The **Recent quotes** section displays current information about the stocks you have looked at recently. If you are signed in to Google any portfolios you have created will be shown here as well.

Recent quotes			
Name	Price	Change	MktCap
VOD	141.40	-2.80 (-1.94%)	74,753.95M
RBS	236.50	-5.00 (-2.07%)	38,136.61M
HSBA	877.25	-10.25 (-1.15%)	105,936.88M
BARC	353.75	-10.00 (-2.75%)	28,769.97M
LLOY	304.00	-7.00 (-2.25%)	17,507.05M
TSCO	393.50	-3.00 (-0.76%)	30,897.44M
BAY	272.75	-0.50 (-0.18%)	3,156.65M
BP Tesco PLC	.00	+0.50 (0.10%)	95,880.01M

Fig. 6.5 Recent Quotes

If you move the pointer over a stock's ticker symbol (in the **Name** column), the full name will show in a message box, as shown above for our favourite supermarket. If you click the **Name** link its page of current detailed data will be opened.

Sector Summary

You can see at a glance how the major sectors are currently performing in the London financial markets. Scrolling over the bar charts will show you more detailed information about percentage increases and decreases for a given sector, as we show in Fig. 6.6.

To get more detail on a sector, simply click its name to open its data page. This will show details of all the LSE companies in the sector, the top moving shares, related news articles and an interactive chart comparing the sector results with the FTSE 100 index.

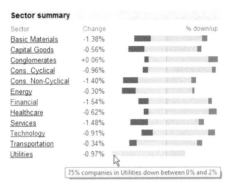

Fig. 6.6 LSE Sector Summary

Trends

Trends | Price | Mkt Cap | Vol

Gainers	Change	Mkt Cap
Wellstream Holdings PLC	2.28%	1,161.83M
Informa plc	1.52%	1,910.82M
easyJet plc	1.38%	1,624.21M
BP plc	1.22%	97,051.56M
Rentokil Initial plc	0.99%	1,383.81M

Losers	Change	Mkt Cap
Enterprise Inns plc	-13.67%	1,342.11M
Mitchells & Butlers plc	-7.51%	1,132.52M
Alliance & Leicester Plc	-6.76%	1,334.59M
Whitbread plc	-6.09%	1,907.49M
Kazakhmys plc	-5.91%	5,962.58M

Excludes stocks with mkt cap less than £1,000M. See FAQ

Fig. 6.7 The Trends Section

The **Trends** section allows you to see which companies are currently the biggest gainers and losers in terms of:

Price – % price change compared to the previous day.

Mkt Cap (Market Capitalisation) – change in market capitalisation, or the market value of the company, compared to the previous day.

Volume – lists the stocks with the highest traded volume.

Company Searches

With Google Finance you can search for stocks, mutual funds or unit trusts, and public companies, using the **Get quotes** entry box described on page 66.

A list of the exchanges and indices covered by Google Finance is given in Appendix B. At the time of writing, quotations were real-time for the New York Stock Exchange and NASDAQ in the US, but the other International markets had time delays of between 10 and 20 minutes.

To look at the results of such a search see **G20**. This shows an enormous amount of information in colour. The 20 minute delayed share price is shown in the top left corner, with other trading and ratio details. Below is a chart correlating market data with corresponding dated news stories to help you determine if there was a relationship between them. In our example, news item **D** is highlighted both on the graph and in the news list, and could have been the reason the share price went up at that time. You can also click and drag the chart to see different time periods and zoom out to see results for a longer period of time.

As well as **News**, there are tabs for **Blogs** and **Feeds**. We will leave it to you to have fun with these.

The **Related Companies** shown are the ones Google considers to be similar in some way, so that you can make quick comparisons. Next to it in **Discussions**, Google Finance offers quality Discussion groups with moderators to keep conversations "lively and spam-free".

The **Summary** includes a précis history of the company, its aims and contact details. The **Officers and directors** section lists key personnel and sometimes even puts a face to a name. When you place your cursor over an executive name, that person's details are displayed, as shown in **G20**. If a photograph is available it is shown here.

We think this is more than enough information to let you make informed judgements on whether to buy, sell or keep a company's shares.

Tracking Currencies

Google Finance offers data on how leading currencies are performing against each other. You can click a particular currency's link on the home page, such as GBP-USD, to go to a page with a history chart, relevant news, and current exchange rates for the main financial currencies, as shown in Fig. 6.8 below.

British Pound (GBP) in United States Dollar (USD)

1 GBP = **1.779 USD** -0.0015 (-0.084%) Sep 3, 5:00PM - View USD in GBP

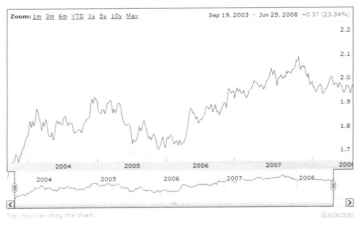

1 GBP in other currencies:

Japanese Yen	¥ 192.492 JPY -1.1284 (-0.583%)	Euro	€ 1.228 EUR +0.0003 (0.027%)
Swiss Franc	1.967 CHF -0.0042 (-0.214%)	Australian Dollar	$ 2.131 AUD +0.0025 (0.119%)
Canadian Dollar	$ 1.887 CAD -0.0171 (-0.897%)	Indian Rupee	78.196 INR -0.8092 (-1.024%)

Fig. 6.8 Currency Exchange Rates and Conversion

There is also a very useful currency converter at the bottom of the page, which lets you easily convert between most of the main currencies worldwide. This obviously uses the currently available exchange rates.

Your Own Portfolios

Google Finance lets you create and maintain portfolios of shares and mutual funds. This helps you to keep track of your investments and instantly know their actual value. It also gives you access to relevant financial information such as news and company management details. You can have as many portfolios in Google Finance as you like, with each holding up to 200 transactions.

To create a portfolio you need to be signed in to a Google Account (see page 31). Then you can click the **Portfolio** link at the top of the Google Finance page, as we did below.

Portfolios - My Portfolio   Create new portfolio

My Portfolio - Edit portfolio

This portfolio is empty. Add a stock or a mutual fund.

Information that you enter will be stored in your Google Account. Please see our Privacy Policy for more information and the Help Centre to learn how to edit and delete information.

Add - Basics | Transactions

Symbol(s) (Comma-separated)   Shares (Optional)   Price (Optional)

ba| 500   420   Add to portfolio

BA	BAE Systems plc
BAC	Bank of America Corporation
BATS	British American Tobacco plc
BAYRY	Bayer AG (ADR)
BASFY	BASF SE (ADR)
BARC	Barclays PLC
BA	The Boeing Company
BAX	Baxter International Inc.
BAM.A	Brookfield Asset Management Inc.

Canada - 中国版 (China)

ly, not for trading purposes or advice and may be

se see disclaimer.

Fig. 6.9 Creating a First Portfolio

From here you just plough straight in and add the transactions you want to show. If you want Google Finance to work out total values, etc., of your portfolio, each transaction needs details of at least the number of **Shares** and their **Price** (enter this in pence, not pounds), as shown in Fig. 6.9. If you just want to watch a share, you can leave these blank. Finally click the **Add to portfolio** button.

You can also add a company or fund to your portfolio by clicking the **Add to Portfolio** link at the top of a stock search result page.

Name	Symbol	Last price	Change	Shares	Cost basis	Mkt value	Gain	Gain %	Day's gain
Barclays PLC	BARC	344.50*	-5.75 (-1.64%)	500.00	2,100.00	1,727.50	-372.50	-17.74%	-23.75
Tesco PLC	TSCO	384.60*	-3.40 (-0.88%)	1,200.00	3,744.00	4,618.80	874.80	23.37%	-37.20
J Sainsbury plc	SBRY	358.00*	+3.00 (0.85%)						
BP plc	BP	523.75*	+17.75 (3.51%)						
					£5,844.00	£6,346.30	£502.30	8.60%	-£60.95

My Portfolio - Overview | Fundamentals | **Performance** | Transactions | Edit transactions - portfolio | Download to spreadsheet

* Indicates a delay of up to 20 minutes - Disclaimer

Fig. 6.10 My Portfolio with a Few Transactions Entered

Here we have added two stock holdings, and two we want to track, to the default **My Portfolio**. Fig. 6.10 shows the portfolio in **Performance** view. There are three other views you can use, all available on the text menu bar – **Overview**, **Fundamentals**, and **Transactions**.

The **Edit portfolio** option lets you change the sorting of entries within a portfolio, or quickly add or delete portfolio entries, by adding or deleting their ticker names in the text box shown here in Fig. 6.11.

Portfolio Name: My Portfolio

Default currency: British Pound (GBP)

BARC   TSCO   SBRY   BP

Save changes   Cancel

Fig. 6.11 Editing a Portfolio

The **Edit transactions** option lets you add or edit data for specific transactions in the portfolio, such as **Date**, number of **Shares**, **Price** paid for a security, the **Commission** paid or **Notes**. To finalise any changes made you have to click the **Save changes** button.

To delete a portfolio from your account, go to the bottom of either the **Edit transactions** or **Edit portfolio** pages and check the box next to the **Permanently delete this portfolio**

and all transactions stored in it option. Then click the **Delete this portfolio** button.

To add another portfolio to your account, click the **Create new portfolio** link at the top-right of any of the portfolio pages, give the new portfolio a name, and click **OK**.

Good luck using Google Finance, we certainly enjoy it. But lets hope you have more 'luck' with your investments than we do!

7

Google Mail

Google Mail, Gmail for short, is a Web application that allows you to create, send and receive e-mail messages in your browser, and to store them freely and securely on Google's data sites. Your e-mail messages are then accessible to you at any time from anywhere.

Advantages of Gmail

As Gmail is designed around Google's search technology and its vast storage capability, it is easy to:

- Search your e-mail messages to find exactly what you want quickly and efficiently provided you archive rather than delete them. Google automatically groups each message with all its replies and displays them as a 'conversation'.

- Keep all your e-mail messages – no need to delete messages to keep them manageable, as Google allows you around 7,000 MB of storage, of which more than 2,600 MB is reserved for e-mail messages.

- Filter all messages for spam so you don't have to worry on that score. If a spam e-mail happens to get through, all you have to do is mark it and press the **Report Spam** link at the top of the message screen. This gives valuable information to the Google team working on spam blocking.

You might be asking yourself "how is it possible to do all this without paying?". The answer, of course, is 'contextual ads'. These are text ads similar to those appearing to the right of Google search results. Thus the service is free to you!

Signing up for a Google Account

Signing up for a Google personal account is very easy. This procedure is required if you hope to access any of the programs that deal with your personal data, such as e-mail messages or your own documents.

Start Google and point to **Mail**. When the mouse pointer changes to a hand, as shown in Fig. 7.1, click the left mouse button.

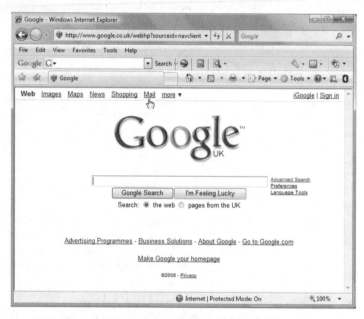

Fig. 7.1 Starting Google Mail in the Windows Explorer Browser

This opens the screen shown in Fig. 7.2 on the next page, in which you are asked to either 'Sign in' if you already have a Google account, or 'Sign up' if this is the first time you have logged onto this Web page.

Fig. 7.2 The Sign in or Sign up Screen

To create a Google account simply point to the **Sign up for Google Mail**, as shown above, and provide the required information, detailed below.

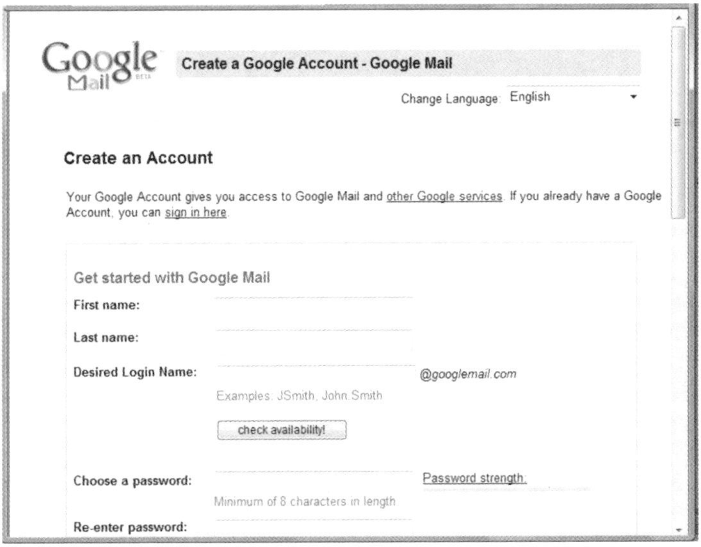

Fig. 7.3 Signing up into a Google Account

You'll have to scroll down to enter additional information, such as Security Questions, Secondary e-mail address (in case you forget your password so it can be sent to you), Location, and Word verification. Once these are supplied your account with Gmail and other personal applications with Google is generated and the screen shown in Fig. 7.4 is displayed.

Fig. 7.4 The Gmail Account Congratulations Screen

After reading the information on this page, click the **I'm ready – show me my account** link at the top of the page to open your account which contains a message from the Google Mail Team, shown in Fig. 7.5. It is worth spending some time reading what they have to offer by following the links to **Getting Started**, **Import your contacts**, and **Setup your mobile phone**.

Next time you start Gmail or any of Google's other personal applications, such as Google Docs, you will be asked to provide your chosen Username and Password.

The Gmail Screen

The Gmail screen showing the first received e-mail message from the Gmail team is shown below.

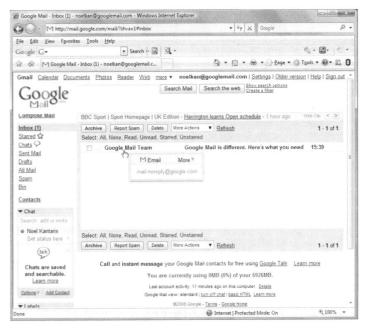

Fig. 7.5 The Gmail Team's Message

As you can see in the above screen, if you let your mouse pointer hover over the sender's address, a box is displayed containing two options; the e-mail address of the person who sent you the message, and the **More** option.

To access the two options within this box your mouse pointer must be placed well within the middle of the sender's address, otherwise as you move the mouse pointer towards the two options, the displayed box disappears.

Clicking the **Email** option opens a new mail screen with the address inserted into the **To:** box, while clicking the **More** option displays any recent conversations (see next section) you might have had with this person.

What is Different

Apart from being Web based, the main difference between Google Mail and other e-mail programs like Windows Mail, Outlook Express and Outlook, is that it automatically groups all your e-mails with their answers into 'Conversations' (discussed later) so you don't have to organise your received e-mails into different folders.

Thus, provided you don't delete any e-mails (but archive them instead), it is easy to find any e-mail you sent and it is then displayed together with all the answers you received on the subject. What a fantastic concept! Furthermore, a single conversation can have several labels, so if a conversation covers more than one topic, you can retrieve it with any of the labels that you have applied to it.

The other program options available on the left of the Gmail screen, when you left-click them, are:

Fig. 7.6 Gmail Options

Compose Mail – Opens a new Gmail form for you to type a new e-mail.

Inbox – Returns a list of received e-mail messages. The number in brackets next to the **Inbox**, (if any), indicates the number of unread messages.

Starred – Displays a list of your starred e-mail messages. To star a message, click the light blue star beside any message or conversation to give it a special status and make it easier to find later.

Chats – Displays a history of your chats. Whether this history is saved or not is controlled from the **Settings** option to be found at the top of Gmail's screen. Gmail's chat features allow you to make free voice calls by connecting you to the **Google Talk** network.

Sent Mail – Displays a list of messages you have sent.

Drafts – Displays a list of messages you have not sent. These are saved in **Drafts**, for you to edit or send.

All Mail – Displays all the messages you have received, sent, or archived, but not those you have deleted.

Spam – Displays all e-mail messages that have been marked as spam.

Bin – Displays all the e-mail messages you have deleted. Having looked at these, you can left-click the **Empty Bin now** option to remove deleted messages permanently. Messages left in the **Bin** for more than 30 days are deleted automatically.

To see the **Inbox** screen in colour, after several e-mail messages have been received, have a look at **G21** in Colour Gallery 1.

Contacts

The Gmail **Contacts** list allows you to store addresses, phone numbers, e-mail addresses and notes for all your contacts. By clicking on a contact you can view more information and all your conversations with that person. Whenever you send an e-mail to someone, their e-mail address is added to your **Contacts** list automatically.

Gmail allows you to import your **Contacts** list from several e-mail programs, such as Yahoo!, Hotmail, Outlook and Outlook Express, orkut, AOL, and others. To achieve this do the following:

- Open your old e-mail program, go to the **Contacts** list then export the contacts (in Outlook this is done from the **File** menu option) into a 'Comma Separated Values' (CSV) file format.

- In Gmail, click the **Contacts** option and then the **Import** link at the top right of the screen, as shown in Fig. 7.7 on the next page.

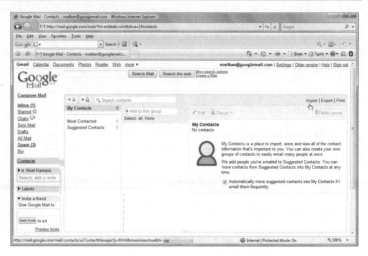

Fig. 7.7 Importing a Contact List

- Next, locate the .CSV file you exported your contacts to from your old e-mail program and double-click it. Your contacts will now be imported into Gmail.

The e-mail addresses of new people who send you a message are added automatically into your **Contacts** if you reply to their message. Alternatively, you can add a new contact manually by left-clicking the **New Contact** link shown in Fig. 7.8 below.

Fig. 7.8 Adding a New Contact

This opens a form to the right of the screen, under **My Contacts** in Fig. 7.8, in which you type the name, e-mail address, phone number, etc., of a new contact then click **Save** to add the new contact to the **Contacts** list.

You can also edit an existing contact by double-clicking its entry in the **Contacts** list, then clicking the **Edit** link, after making changes click the **Save** link as shown in Fig. 7.9. You can even add a picture of the person, if you happen to have one, or click the **Delete contact** link to remove this contact from your **Contacts** list.

Fig. 7.9 Editing a Contact

Conversation View

The concept of 'Conversations' is unique to Gmail. It groups automatically all e-mail messages with their answers so that you can see at a glance who said what in such exchanges.

To illustrate a conversation, let us take a closer look at part of our **Inbox**, shown in Fig. 7.10.

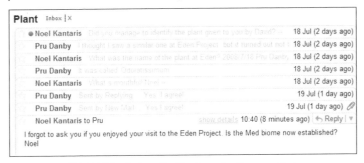

Fig. 7.10 An Automatic Stacking of a Conversation

Here we started an exchange of e-mail messages between Noel and Pru under the subject **Plant**. As both participants replied to the messages they received Gmail automatically stacked them all under the heading **Plant**.

The penultimate message was sent twice; once by replying to the recipient, and a second time by clicking the link **Compose Message** and sending it as a new message. As you can see, both messages, no matter which way they were sent, were incorporated by Gmail into the same conversation, provided the subject line was the same.

To see the subtle differences in colour between originator of the conversation and the various replies, see **G22** where the **Show Details** link on the last message was also clicked. Note that although this last message was sent by Google mail, as shown at the bottom of the screen, the **from** entry shows a different e-mail address from that used in Gmail – more about this shortly!

Using Labels

You can add more than one label to a message or conversation. Labels help you to organise your e-mail messages in a much better way than the traditional 'Folders' in conventional e-mail programs. For example:

In the past you might have used a 'Jokes' folder to keep all the e-mail messages which had some kind of joke attached to them. You might also have used a 'Family' folder to keep all the messages from various members of your family, and yet another folder to keep all messages dealing with 'Legal' matters. However, if a message arrived from a family member containing serious legal matters, but also had a joke attached to it, in which folder would you keep it?

With Gmail's 'Labels' you simply attach three labels to such a message: 'Jokes', 'Family' and 'Legal'.

So now, using Gmail, you can retrieve all the 'Family' messages, amongst which there will also be the one with the attached joke and legal matters, while retrieving all the 'Jokes' will also bring forth the one from your family joker, etc. This is a much more flexible way of categorising your e-mail messages than using the old folder system!

Creating a Label

To create a label do the following:

- Click the **Settings** link at the top of the Gmail screen (pointed to in Fig. 7.11), then in the **Settings** screen click the **Labels** link, also shown in Fig. 7.11. This opens the **Labels** screen shown in Fig. 7.12 below, for you to type the new label in the text box provided, then click the **Create** link to the right of the text box to complete the operation.

- Repeat to create as many labels as you require.

Fig. 7.11 The Settings Screen

Fig. 7.12 Creating a New Label

- Next, select the message(s) by clicking the small square on the left of each, then click the **More Actions** link at the top of the screen and select the required label from the drop-down list (see Fig. 7.13).

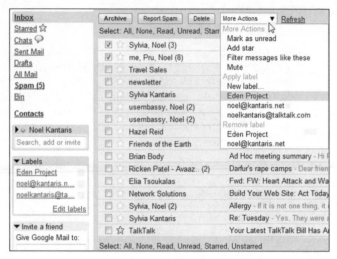

Fig. 7.13 Allocating a Label to E-mail Message(s)

What happens next, is that a message appears at the top of the screen telling you how many conversations you have selected.

Now, clicking the label 'Eden Project' on the left of the screen under the **Labels** link, displays all the e-mail messages that have been so labelled, as shown in Fig. 7.14. You can also allocate colours to labels, as shown in **G23**.

Fig. 7.14 A list of Labelled E-mail Messages

Archiving E-mail Messages

To keep your **Inbox** tidy, messages that have been allocated all the appropriate labels, can be archived by clicking the small squares to the left of each message to select it, then clicking **Archive**, as shown in Fig. 7.15.

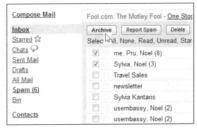

Fig. 7.15 Archiving Selected Messages

If someone responds to messages that have been archived, those messages and their corresponding conversations will reappear in your **Inbox**.

Archived messages can be found in the **All Mail** list by selecting an appropriate label or searching for them. To move archived messages into the **Inbox**, do the following:

- In the **All Mail** list, select them and click the **Move to Inbox** button, as shown in Fig. 7.16.

Fig. 7.16 Moving Messages from the All Mail List

- Locate them by either searching for them or by selecting an appropriate label, then click the **More Actions** button and choose **Move to Inbox** from the drop-down list of actions, as shown in Fig. 7.17.

Fig. 7.17 Moving E-mail from a Search or Label List

Using Filters

Filters allow you to dictate what happens to incoming messages in Gmail. You can use filters to automatically forward, star, label, archive, or delete mail arriving in your **Inbox**, based on the sender's address, or any combination of keywords. You can create a filter, as follows:

- Click the **Create a filter** link at the top of any Gmail screen, shown in Fig. 7.18.

Fig. 7.18 The Create a Filter Link

- In the displayed screen, shown in Fig. 7.19 below, enter your filter criteria in the appropriate fields.

Fig. 7.19 Creating a Filter

- To see which messages currently in Gmail match your filter conditions, click the **Test Search** button. Next, you can either update your criteria and run another test search, or click the **Next Step** button to display a screen of actions that can be applied to messages that meet your chosen criteria.

- Finally, select one or more actions from the list which will be applied in the order in which these actions are listed. For example, you could choose to **Forward** matching messages to a specified e-mail address, then **Delete** them.

As an example we chose to search for all messages whose e-mail address is usembassy@------.com.

We then create a filter to send all such incoming e-mail messages to a certain recipient, then have them deleted from our **Inbox**. The search results and proposed filter are shown in Fig. 7.20 in which we also chose to apply the filter results to all the messages in Gmail by checking the box **Also apply filter to 2 conversations below**.

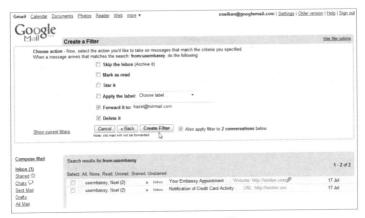

Fig. 7.20 Designing a Filter

- To complete the operation, click the **Create Filter** box.

From now on the filter takes effect and all messages from the specified e-mail address will be forwarded, then deleted.

Receiving Mail from Multiple Addresses

Lots of people have multiple e-mail addresses; one on their Web site, one in Hotmail, and another in Gmail. Wouldn't it be ideal if all e-mail messages from these addresses could come into your Gmail box? The answer is 'yes', it can.

Furthermore, each time someone replies to a message you send using a custom **From:** address, the reply will be delivered to the **From:** address rather than your GMail address. Here is how:

Sign-in to your Gmail account, click the **Settings** link at the top of the screen, then click the **Accounts** link, followed by the **Add another e-mail address** link, as shown in Fig. 7.21 below.

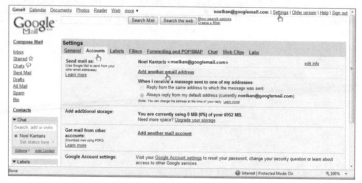

Fig. 7.21 The Settings, Account Screen

This opens a separate window in which you are asked to enter your additional e-mail address, as shown in Fig. 7.22.

Fig. 7.22 The Add Another E-mail Address Screen

You can also specify here that replies to your message should be delivered to a specified e-mail address rather than your GMail address. If you would like replies to be delivered to another account, click the **Specify a different "reply-to"** link and enter the address in the box that opens up. You might, for example, like to train your friends to send you mail to only one address. On the other hand, you might really like to confuse them by changing your return e-mail address, which in Gmail you can do 'on the fly', by clicking the down arrow next to the **From:** box and selecting one of your other e-mail addresses!

Composing a New Message

To compose and send a new message, click the **Compose Mail** link. This opens the screen shown in Fig. 7.23.

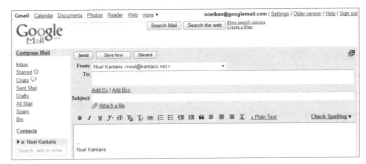

Fig. 7.23 The New Mail Screen

In the **To:** box you type the recipient's e-mail address. If the recipient is in your **Contacts** list, then typing the first letter of a name will list all addresses starting with that letter. All you have to do is choose the appropriate one.

The best way to test out any unfamiliar e-mail features is to send a test message to your own e-mail address. This saves wasting somebody else's time, and the message can be very quickly checked to see the results.

Next, type a title for the message in the **Subject:** box. The text in this subject field will form a header for the message when it is received, so it helps to show in a few words what the message is about. Finally, type your message and click the **Send** button shown here.

Message Formatting

Gmail provides quite sophisticated formatting options for an e-mail editor. All the formatting features are self-explanatory. If you hover the mouse pointer over any one of these, a text message is displayed telling you of its function, while left-clicking one, either actions the formatting or displays options to choose from.

You should be able to prepare some very easily readable e-mail messages with these features, but remember that not everyone will be able to read the work in the way that you spent hours creating. Only e-mail programs that support MIME (Multipurpose Internet Mail Extensions) can read such formatting (referred to as HTML formatting). When your recipient's e-mail program does not read HTML, and many people choose not to, the message appears as plain text with an HTML file attached.

Using E-mail Attachments

If you want to include an attachment with your main e-mail message, you simply click the **Attach a file** link, under the **Subject** box, which opens a separate window displaying your Desktop, from which you can navigate to the file you want to attach. This could be a document, a photo, or indeed a video.

When you receive a message with an attachment, it displays with a paper clip to the right of it, as shown in Fig. 7.24 below.

Fig. 7.24 A Received Message with Attachment

Hovering the mouse pointer on the paper clip displays the name and type of the attachment. In our example the attachment contains two **.jpg** photos.

Right-clicking the attachment displays a choice of options, amongst which is the ability to save the attachment into an appropriate folder on your hard disc.

Left-clicking the e-mail or the attachment, opens the actual e-mail message with a paper clip icon displayed at the top right of the screen. Left-clicking the paper clip now opens the attachment (in this example the two photos) and places them just below the e-mail message so that you can see them and decide whether you would like to save them or not.

Gmail on your Mobile

To configure your mobile phone (we demonstrate the procedure using a Nokia smart phone) to use Gmail, do the following:

- Use the **Menu** option on your mobile to select the **Web**, as shown in **G24**. If images similar to the ones shown here are not displayed, then you may have to upgrade your mobile before you can access the Internet.

- In your Web browser enter the string **m.google.com** and select the **Search** option. What appears on your screen is shown in **G25**.

- Scroll down to the **Google, *Tip: Bookmark this page for quick access** entry as shown, and select it.

- Scroll down to **Gmail** as shown in **G26**, and select it.

- Select the **Visit Now** entry and, when offered the choice, select to go directly to the page.

- On the displayed **Gmail** screen, select the **Get faster Gmail** entry, as shown in **G27**. This downloads the newer and faster version of the program and installs it on your mobile, usually in the **Apps** menu option.

- From now on to receive your e-mail messages, answer them, or create new ones on the go, simply navigate to the **Apps** menu option of your mobile, select it, and scroll down to the **Google Mail** option, as shown in **G28**.

As you can see in **G29**, the contents of the **Inbox** are almost identical to those when using your PC. So now, there is no need to feel deprived when you are away from your computer! However, do keep an eye on the cost of the service, as this can be rather excessive with some providers, particularly when answering e-mails.

We use our mobiles to check our e-mail while overseas. No need to visit Internet cafes for that. On a recent trip to Europe, each access to our Inbox cost less than 10p.

Getting Help with Gmail

Whenever you need to know anything, help is at hand. Simply click the **Help** link shown in Fig. 7.25 and a separate screen is displayed, as shown in Fig. 7.26.

Fig. 7.25 The Help Link

Fig. 7.26 The Help Screen, shown in the Google Chrome Browser

On this screen, you can either type your query in the text box labelled **What can we help you with?**, or you can use any of the other links to look for an answer. You can also use the links under **Troubleshooting** or those under **Recommended articles**. Also, if you scroll down the **Help** page you'll find links to additional topics. We found the **Help** system of Google Mail extremely thorough.

8

Google Documents

As we have already seen, search-related activities are only part of what is offered by Google on the Web. Google now offers Web based applications as alternatives to traditional desktop software, for word processing, spreadsheets and presentations, to name but a few. To access these you must have an account with Google (see page 31).

Cloud Computing

Google Docs (or Documents) is Web-based software available to you free of charge. It is accessed with your Web browser, which is probably either Google Chrome, Microsoft Internet Explorer or Firefox. This new approach to running software, which is not actually on your PC, but 'in the ether', has been dubbed by the media as 'Cloud Computing'.

As your documents are all saved online they are not only accessible to you, for editing maybe, from anywhere, but are also available to nominated colleagues for collaboration.

Google Docs has three main components:

- **Documents** – for word processing. Each document file is limited to 500 KB in size plus up to 2 MB per embedded image.

- **Spreadsheets** – with each file being limited to 256 columns. However, the overall limit is 200,000 cells (50,000 cells with formulae) or 100 sheets – whichever is reached first. There is no limit on rows.

- **Presentations** – in .ppt and .pps formats are limited to 10 MB each, with an overall limit of 5,000 documents and 5,000 images.

When you first action **Documents** from the **more** drop-down

options in Google, as shown in Fig. 8.1, the sign-in screen is displayed as shown in Fig. 8.2 below. However, this screen is not shown if you are already signed in <u>and</u> you action Google Documents from within that Google application.

Fig. 8.1 Starting Google
Documents

Fig. 8.2 The Documents Welcome Screen

It is worthwhile spending some time with **Taking a tour**, and examining the various options under **New Features**. You can even spend a little time running the video "Google Docs in Plain English".

Uploading Existing Documents

You can upload existing documents, whether word processed Documents, Spreadsheets, or Presentations, provided they conform to the following file formats:

> **Documents** – HTML, Plain text (.txt), Microsoft Word (.doc), .rtf, Open Office (.odt).
>
> **Spreadsheets** – xls, csv, ods, txt, tsv or tsb.
>
> **Presentations** – .ppt and .pps.

Google Docs also supports .jpg image files and Adobe .pdf files.

Note: At present Google Documents does not support the latest file formats used by Microsoft Office 2007, such as .docx, .xlsx, and .pptx. If you want to upload such files, use the application that created them and save the files in a pre-2007 file format.

To upload a file, simply left-click the **Upload** option at the top of the **Documents** screen, pointed to in Fig. 8.3 below.

Fig. 8.3 The Documents Upload Option

This displays the screen in Fig. 8.4 shown on the next page.

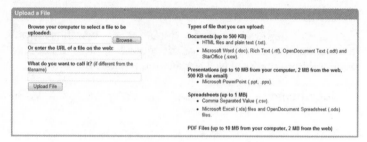

Fig. 8.4 The Documents Upload Screen

On this screen you can use the **Browse** facility to locate and select the file you want to upload, give it a different name, if you want, then click the **Upload File** button to send it to a Google server.

As an example, we have uploaded four existing files; a Project Spreadsheet, a Training Presentation, a Memo to PC Users Word document, and a Family Background pdf.

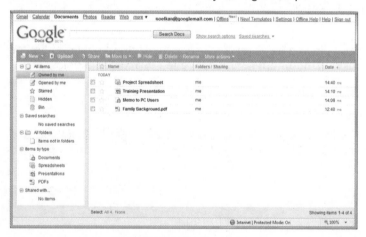

Fig. 8.5 Uploaded Documents

Note, that when you have lots of different documents uploaded, you can choose to display them by type by clicking the appropriate option at the left bottom of the above screen; Documents, Spreadsheets, Presentation, or PDFs.

Sharing Documents

You can select one or more of your documents and share them with nominated colleagues. All you have to do is select the documents, then click on the **Share** button (pointed to in Fig. 8.6 below), which opens the **Add collaborators or viewers** window, which is also shown in Fig. 8.6.

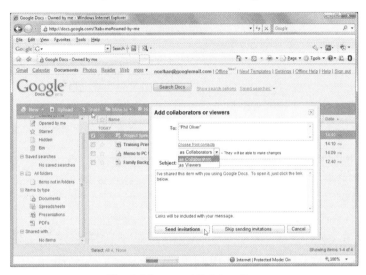

Fig. 8.6 Document Collaboration

In the **To:** box, you either type the e-mail addresses of the people you want to share your documents with, or you can click the **Choose from contacts** link to select one or more people who are already in your **Contacts** list.

Next, choose between the two options; **as Collaborators** or **as Viewers**, and click the **Send Invitations** button. Collaborators can make changes to the shared documents, while Viewers can only view them.

As an example the **Memo to PC Users** was sent to a colleague as a collaborator, who was then able to add some formatting to it. The changes to such a document could then be viewed by the originator and any other invited person sharing his document.

Removing Collaborators

At any time, the originator of a document can remove other

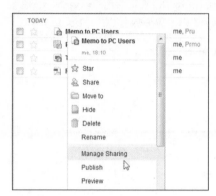

collaborators by right-clicking the document under question to display the drop-down menu shown in Fig. 8.7. As it can also be seen, collaborators' initials appear next to the document list.

Fig. 8.7 The Right-click Menu of a Document

Left-clicking the **Manage Sharing** option, displays the contents of Fig. 8.8.

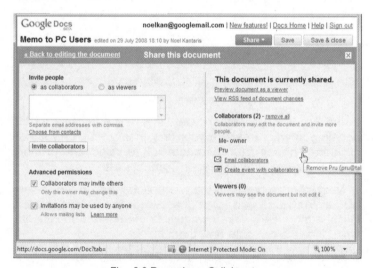

Fig. 8.8 Removing a Collaborator

Left-clicking the small square ⊠, pointed to above, removes the relevant collaborator.

Creating Documents from Scratch

 Google Docs offers you the ability to create various types of documents from scratch. For the rest of this chapter and for the following two, we introduce the various applications you use to do this.

Word Processing

To start a word processed document from scratch, select the **New**, **Document** menu option which displays the screen in Fig. 8.10 below.

Note that apart from the options to create the three types of documents, the drop-down menu also offers you the ability to create a **Folder**. As you accumulate a large number of documents, it is a good idea to create separate folders to hold the three different type of documents.

Fig. 8.9 The New
Document Menu
Option

The drop-down menu also offers you the ability to create a document **From template**. It is worth while looking at these templates as you might find one that saves you a lot of time in designing and formatting your own.

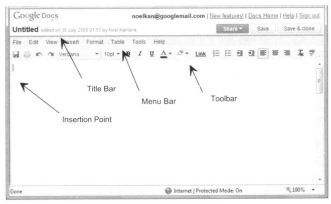

Fig. 8.10 The Google Docs Document Screen

Note that in this case, the document window displays an empty document with the title shown as 'Untitled'.

The Menu Bar Options

Each menu bar option has associated with it a pull-down

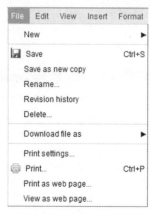

sub-menu. Left-clicking a Menu bar option, reveals the pull-down sub-menu associated with it. Fig. 8.11 shows the sub-menu commands of the **File** option which are largely self-explanatory.

Some of the sub-menu commands can be accessed with 'quick key' combinations from the keyboard. Such combinations are shown on the drop-down menus. For example, **Ctrl+S** is the quick key for the **Save** option in the **File** sub-menu. If a sub-menu option

Fig. 8.11 The File Sub-menu

is not available at any time, it will display in a grey colour. If you like keyboard shortcuts, have a look at **Help**, **Keyboard shortcuts** where you'll find a rather large list.

Shortcut Menus

Context-sensitive shortcut menus are also extremely useful features. If you click the right mouse button on any screen feature, or document, a shortcut menu is displayed with the most frequently used commands relating to the type of work you were doing at the time.

The composite screen dump in Fig. 8.12 displayed on the next page shows in turn the shortcut menus that open when selected text, or the Menu bar area is right-clicked. In the first shortcut menu the **Cut** and **Copy** commands only become effective if you have some text selected.

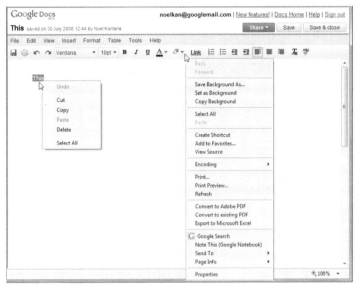

Fig. 8.12 Example Shortcut Menus.

Left-clicking the mouse on an open menu selection will choose that function, while clicking on an area outside the shortcut menu (or pressing the **Esc** key), closes down the shortcut menu.

Entering Text

In order to illustrate some word processing capabilities, you need to have a short text at hand. We suggest you select the **New**, **Document** menu option and type the memo displayed on the next page in Fig. 8.13. Don't worry if the length of the lines in our example differ from those on your display.

As you type in text, any time you want to force a new line, or paragraph, just press **Enter**. While typing within a paragraph, the word processor sorts out line lengths automatically (known as 'word wrap'), without you having to press any keys to move to a new line. If you make a mistake while typing, press the **BkSp** key enough times to erase it and start again.

MEMO TO PC USERS
Networked Computers
The microcomputers in the Data Processing room are a mixture of
IBM compatible PCs with Intel Centrino Duo processors running at
various speeds. Most have CD-ROM drives, while the latest
machines are equipped with DVD drives of 4.7 GB capacity. The PCs
are connected to various printers via a network; the Laser printers
available giving best output.

The computer you are using will have at least a 100 GB capacity hard
disc on which a number of software programs, including the latest
version of Windows, have been installed. To make life easier, the
hard disc is highly structured with each program installed in a
separate folder.

Fig. 8.13 Sample Text Entered in a New Document

You can move the cursor around a document with the
normal direction keys, and with the key combinations listed
below.

To move	*Press*
Left one character	⇐
Right one character	⇒
Up one line	⇑
Down one line	⇓
Left one word	Ctrl+ ⇐
Right one word	Ctrl+ ⇒
To beginning of line	Home
To end of line	End
To paragraph beginning	Ctrl+ ⇑
To paragraph end	Ctrl+ ⇓
Up one screen	PgUp
Down one screen	PgDn
To beginning of file	Ctrl+Home
To end of file	Ctrl+End

Changing Paragraph Styles

To change the style of a paragraph, first place the insertion pointer in the paragraph, say the title line of the memo, then click the **Format** button on the Menu bar (see Fig. 8.14), and select the **Heading (H1)** option from the drop-down menu. The selected paragraph reformats instantly to the new style.

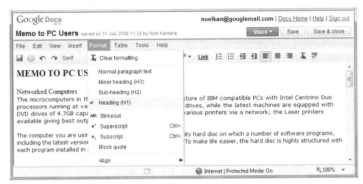

Fig. 8.14 Changing the Formatting of a Paragraph

Now with the insertion pointer in the second line of text, select **Sub-heading (H2)** which reformats the line in Serif 14pt.

Document Screen Displays

This Word processor provides three display views; **Fixed-width page** (shown in Fig. 8.15), **Normal** (shown in Fig. 8.14), and **Full-screen**. How you work, is your choice.

Fig. 8.15 The View Menu

Editing and Formatting Text

For small deletions, such as letters or words, the easiest method is to use the **Del** or **BkSp** keys.

When larger scale editing is needed you have several alternatives. You could first 'select' the text to be altered (see below), then use the **Cut, Copy** and **Paste** buttons, shown here, and available in the **Edit** sub-menu. Alternatively, you could use the quick key combinations, **Ctrl+C** to copy, and **Ctrl+V** to paste. These operations are carried out via the system Clipboard.

To select text with the keyboard, position the insertion pointer on the first character to be selected and hold down the **Shift** key while using the arrow keys to highlight the required text, then release the **Shift** key.

To select text with the mouse, press down the left mouse button at the beginning of the block and while holding it pressed, drag the cursor across the block so that the desired text is highlighted, then release the mouse button.

Once text has been selected it can be copied to another location in your present document, to another type of Google document, or to another Windows application.

To change our memo into what appears in Fig. 8.17 on the next page, first select the title of the memo and format it to 18 point size Comic Sans MS by selecting it from the drop-down **Font** box shown in Fig. 8.16 to the left. Next change it into italics and centre it between the margins using the two Toolbar buttons shown here. Similarly, change the subtitle to 14 point size and each paragraph of the main body to 12 point size Comic Sans MS.

Fig. 8.16 The Font Types

Note that both title and subtitle are in bold as part of the definition of their respective paragraph style. Also, we found it necessary to remove the formatting from the two paragraphs, using the Toolbar button, shown here, before we could format the main body of the memo.

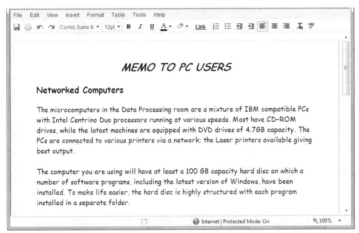

Fig. 8.17 The Reformatted PC Users Memo

All manual formatting, including the selection of font, point size, style (bold, italic, underline), text and background colour, are carried out by first selecting the text and then using the appropriate Toolbar button.

With some actions, such as super/subscript, the easiest way of activating the formatting commands is by using the drop-down menu of the **Format** option of the Menu bar.

Yet another method of formatting text is by using quick keys, some of which are listed below:

To Format	*Type*
Bold	**Ctrl+B**
Italic	**Ctrl+I**
Underline	**Ctrl+U**
Word underline	**Ctrl+Shift+W**

There are quick keys to do almost anything, but the ones listed here are the most useful and the easiest to remember.

Paragraph Alignment

A paragraph is defined as any text which is followed by a paragraph mark, which is created invisibly by pressing the **Enter** key. So single line titles, as well as sections of long typed text, can form paragraphs.

The word processor allows you to align a paragraph at the left margin (the default), at the right margin, centred between both margins, or justified between both margins. As with most operations there are several ways to perform alignment in this word processing program. Three such methods are:

- Using buttons on the **Toolbar**.
- Using keyboard short cuts.
- Using the **Format**, **Align** menu command.

The table below shows the buttons on the Toolbar and their keystroke shortcuts.

Buttons on Toolbar	Paragraph Alignment	Keystrokes
≣	Left	**Ctrl+L**
≣	Centred	**Ctrl+E**
≣	Right	**Ctrl+R**

To justify a paragraph you'll have to use the **Format**, **Align** command and select the last sub-menu option shown here in Fig. 8.18. Alternatively, you could use the keystroke shortcut **Ctrl+J** which is much quicker.

Fig. 8.18 The Justifying Option

Indenting Text

Most documents will require some form of paragraph indenting. An indent is the space between the margin and the edge of the text in the paragraph. When an indent is set, any justification on that side of the page sets at the indent, not the page border.

To illustrate indentation, open the file **Memo to PC Users**, place the insertion pointer in the first paragraph, and then use the second Toolbar button, shown below and in Fig. 8.19, to increase the indent of the paragraph.

Use this button to decrease indent.

Use this button to increase indent.

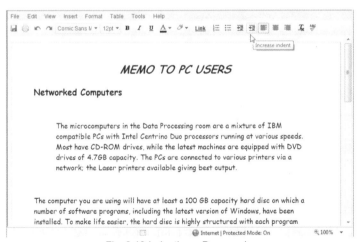

Fig. 8.19 Indenting a Paragraph

The above indentation is known as 'hanging' indentation, where all the lines in a paragraph are indented by the same amount. This is often used in lists to emphasise certain points. To indent only the first line of a paragraph, place the insertion pointer at the beginning of the line and press the tab key.

Using Bullets and Numbered Lists

You can use bullets and numbered lists in the text of your document to improve visual impact. To demonstrate these place the insertion pointer in the first paragraph of the **Memo to PC Users** and click the **Bullet list** Toolbar button pointed to in Fig. 8.20. The paragraph is instantly formatted with a preceding bullet. Below we have repeated the procedure with the second paragraph.

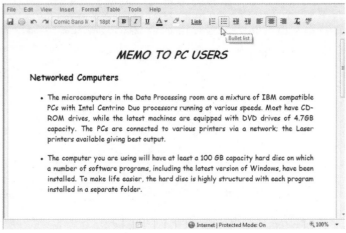

Fig. 8.20 Creating a Bullet List

Pressing the **Enter** key at the end of a paragraph with a bullet, starts the next paragraph with a bullet. To remove bullets from a paragraph, simply place the insertion pointer in the required paragraph and click the **Bullet list** Toolbar button once more.

Numbered lists can be created in a similar manner to bullet lists, but you click the **Numbered list** Toolbar button instead. Pressing the **Enter** key at the end of a numbered paragraph, increases automatically the number preceding the paragraph by one.

To remove a numbered list from a given paragraph, place the insertion pointer in the required paragraph and click the **Numbered List** Toolbar button once more.

Inserting Comments

Another powerful feature of this word processor is the facility

to add comments to a document. Comments are notes, or annotations, that an author or reviewer adds to a document using the **Insert**, **Comment** menu command shown here in Fig. 8.21.

Selecting this command, places the words 'Type here' at the insertion point, followed by the author's or collaborator's name, date and time the comment was inserted, as shown at the bottom of

Fig. 8.21 The Insert
Sub-menu

Fig. 8.22.

Comments can be inserted into the document by left-clicking on the collaborator's name and choosing to do so from the displayed menu shown below. However, you will have to remove the collaborator's name, date and time, manually. Comments that have not been incorporated into a document, do not print to paper.

Fig. 8.22 Inserting a Comment

To make the comment stand out you could change its colour by selecting it and using the **Text Colour** Toolbar button, shown here, which opens a pallet of colours for you to choose from, as shown in **G30**.

Special Characters and Symbols

You can select characters and symbols and insert them into your document using the **Insert, Special characters** command. This opens a window part of which is shown in Fig. 8.23 below.

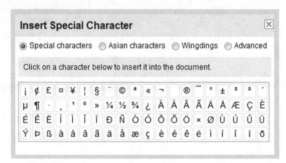

Fig. 8.23 Part of the Insert Special Character Window

You should be able to find just about any character you require in the displayed font. Double-clicking on a character, transfers it to your document at the insertion point.

Clicking the **Wingdings** radio button in the above box displays an amazing number of symbols (part of which are shown below), which can also be inserted into your document by double-clicking.

Fig. 8.24 Part of the Insert Wingdings Window

Using Headers and Footers

To insert a header or footer in a document, click **Insert**, then choose **Header** or **Footer** from the drop-down menu. A text box will appear, where you can type the text for your header or footer. To remove a header or footer, right-click in the text box and choose **Delete header/footer**.

Unlike other word processing programs, page numbering is selected from the **Print Settings** window (see below). Repeated header or footer text only appears on a document when you print it. On the screen you'll only see header text on the first page and footer text on the last page.

Print Settings

To change the print settings, use the **File**, **Print Settings**

command. On the displayed window, you can select the **Paper Size**, whether to print **Page numbers** or not, paper **Orientation** and size of **Margins**.

Fig. 8.25 The Print Settings Window

To print a document, either click the **Print** button in this window, or having set the **Print Settings**, click the **Print** icon on the Toolbar, shown here, to display the **Print** window shown in Fig. 8.26.

In the **Print** window you can select which printer to use (if you have more than one) to print your document, which pages to print, and a host of other choices.

Fig. 8.26 The Print Window

Saving your Document

 Your document is automatically saved to the 'cloud' every few minutes, but you can also force a save by clicking the **Save** Toolbar icon shown here.

Downloading a File

You can also use the **File**, **Download file as** command to download very important files and save them on your computer in several file formats, as shown below. Being able to save a file in PDF format can be useful if you want to e-mail it to colleagues outside the Google environment.

Fig. 8.27 Selecting File Type to Download

* * *

Google's word processor has many more features, far too numerous to mention in the space allocated to this book. What we have tried to do so far, is give you enough basic information so that you can have the confidence to forge ahead and explore the rest of its capabilities by yourself.

* * *

9

Google Spreadsheets

The other type of online document you can use in
Google Docs is a Spreadsheet. As this also uses
'collaboration', we suggest you refer to the beginning
of the previous chapter for a general introduction to Google
Docs.

For us, an uploaded Excel **.xls** spreadsheet with four
worksheets and a consolidation sheet worked fine with all the
cell formatting intact. The only exception were two sheets
with saved charts which were removed by the program. This
is not surprising as the two programs deploy different ways of
creating charts – we shall be discussing Google charts later.

Creating a Spreadsheet

To create a Google spreadsheet from scratch, go to
Documents, click the **New** menu button and select
Spreadsheet from the displayed drop-down menu, as shown
in Fig. 9.1.

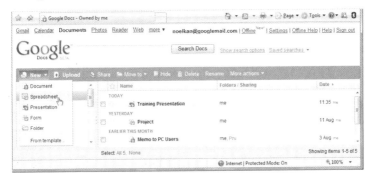

Fig. 9.1 Creating a New Spreadsheet

When you first enter a Google Spreadsheet, it sets up a huge electronic page, or worksheet, in your computer's memory, many times larger than the small part shown on the screen. Individual cells are identified by column and row location (in that order), with the size being limited at present, according to Google, as follows:

- Each Spreadsheet can contain up to 256 columns or up to 200,000 cells or up to 100 sheets – whichever limit is reached first. There is no limit on rows.

- Each Spreadsheet can have up to 50,000 cells with formulas.

- You have a limit of 1,000 Spreadsheets.

- The limit on the number of Spreadsheets that can be opened at the same time is 11.

- You can import Spreadsheets of up to approximately 1 MB in xls, csv, ods, txt, tsv or tsb format.

A Spreadsheet can be thought of as a two-dimensional table made up of rows and columns. The point where a row and column intersect is called a cell, while the reference points of a cell are known as the cell address. The active cell (A1 when you first enter the program) is highlighted.

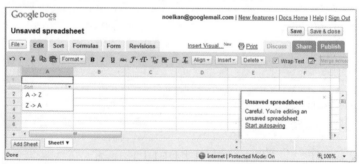

Fig. 9.2 The Edit Toolbar Options

Note that as you hover the mouse pointer just below the first cell of each column, a 'Sort' option appears in red which allows you to sort the contents of columns in ascending or descending order. Also note the **autosaving** option.

Worksheet Navigation

To navigate around a worksheet, use the four arrow keys to move the active cell one position in the direction of the arrow keys or use the **PgDn** and **PgUp** keys to move vertically one full page at a time.

Using the key combination **Ctrl+⇨** moves the active cell to the T column, while **Ctrl+⇩** moves the active cell to the 100th row (these being the initial number of columns and rows on a new worksheet).

Using the key combination **Ctrl+Home** moves the active cell to the A1 position, which is known as the 'Home' position, while **Ctrl+⇦**, moves the active cell to the 1st column of the particular row.

Worksheet Display

When you first start a new worksheet, the **Edit** Menu bar tab is selected which displays the corresponding Toolbar options above the column letters of the worksheet, as shown in Fig. 9.2. Other Menu bar tabs (when selected) display different Toolbar options. The **File** button on the Menu bar, displays a drop-down menu with file related options, allowing you to create a **New** file, **Import** a file, **Open** a file, etc.

Different Toolbar options are displayed when you click the **Formulas** tab, as shown in Fig. 9.3 below.

Fig. 9.3 The Formulas Toolbar

It might be a good idea to click the **Start autosaving** option (see Fig. 9.2) and give the Spreadsheet a name in the **Save** window that displays on your screen. We called ours **Project**. The name of the file then becomes the name of the Spreadsheet and is displayed at the top of the worksheet area, as shown above. We have also typed the words **Project Analysis** in cell A1, as shown above.

The location of the active cell is constantly monitored in the Cell Reference Area at the left end of the **Formulas** Toolbar,

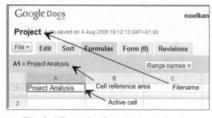

below the Menu bar, as shown in Fig. 9.4. If you type a formula in a cell, pressing **Enter**, causes the actual calculation to appear in the cell, while the actual formula appears in the Cell Reference

Fig. 9.4 Part of a Spreadsheet Screen

Area only when the cell containing the formula is made the active cell <u>and</u> the **Formulas** tab is selected. More about the display of formulas later.

To edit information already in a cell, double-click the cell. The cursor keys, the **Home** and **End** keys, as well as the **Del** key, can be used to move the cursor and/or edit the information displayed in the cell. After such editing, you must press the **Enter** key for changes to take effect.

Adding Borders to a Range of Cells

The looks of a worksheet can be enhanced somewhat by placing lines (or cell borders), to separate information in different rows or columns. To add borders to a cell range, first select it (in our example in Fig. 9.5 we selected A4 to C4 using the keyboard combination **Shift+⇨**), click the **Edit** tab, and select **Borders** from its Toolbar. This displays a drop-down menu (also shown in Fig. 9.5), from which you can place any combination of lines along the borders of selected cells.

To remove border lines from a cell or a range of cells, select them, click the **Borders** icon and click the fourth option (last on the first line).

Fig. 9.5 The Edit Borders Options

Changing Text Alignment and Fonts

Fig. 9.6 Entering Data into a Worksheet.

Note that by default, labels are left-justified, while numbers are right-justified, as shown in columns B and C of row 5 of our example in Fig. 9.6.

To change the text alignment of a range of cells, select the range (B3:C3 in our example), click the **Align** button on the **Edit** tab sheet Toolbar, and select the **Right Align** option shown in Fig. 9.7.

Fig. 9.7 The Format Cells Dialogue Box.

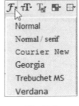

Fig. 9.8

To change the font type of text, such as that in A1, use the **Edit**, **FontFamily** Toolbar option, pointed to in Fig. 9.8, and select a font from the drop-down list. To change font size, use the **Font size** icon, shown here to the right, and select one from the displayed list.

Fig. 9.9 Part of Format List

Finally, since in our example the entered numbers in cells B5 to C5 represent money, select the cell block B5 to C5, and choose the **Format**, **2 Decimals** option from the drop-down list shown in Fig. 9.9.

Changing Column Widths

To change the width of a given column or a number of columns, activate a cell in the relevant column, or select the number of required column cells, then position the mouse pointer in the column headings – it will change shape as you move it over the border of two columns. Dragging this new

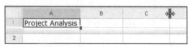

pointer (see Fig. 9.10) right or left, will widen, or narrow, the column or block of columns.

Fig. 9.10 Changing Column Width

In Fig. 9.11 below, we have used a **Zoom** factor (bottom right of the screen) of 150% for clarity – the default being 100%.

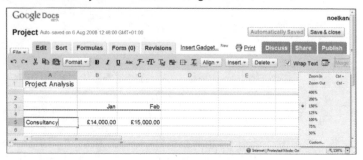

Fig. 9.11 The Formatted Worksheet.

Saving a Spreadsheet

If you have not turned on the **Autosaving** option, you can still save your work by using the **Save & close** button shown in

Fig. 9.12. You will be asked for a filename for the work to be saved under.

Fig. 9.12 The Save & Close Box

In our example, you can clearly see that the **Autosaving** option had been selected earlier. In either case, your document is saved and can be found listed in your Google **Documents**.

Filling in a Worksheet

As an example of how a worksheet can be built up, use the few entries on 'Project Analysis' which we created earlier, or if you haven't done so already, don't worry as you could just as easily start afresh.

When the file is open, double-click existing entries to edit them, or simply retype the contents of cells and format these as we discussed earlier (also see below), so that your worksheet looks like the one in Fig. 9.13. Also note the **Formula Bar** at the bottom of the worksheet, which monitors cell contents irrespective of which tab sheet is active.

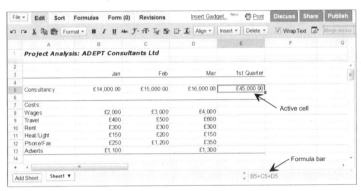

Fig. 9.13 The First Quarter Figures of Adept Consultants

For the contents of row 1 to display as shown, you will have to select columns A to C and click the **Merge across** menu option on the **Edit** tab sheet. We then clicked the **Bold** and **Italic** menu buttons.

The numbers within the cell block B5 to E5 were formatted as **Currency** with 2 decimals, while the numbers within the cell block B8 to E13 were formatted as **Currency** without decimals.

The lines in cells A4 to E4 and A14 to E14 were entered using the **Borders** button and selecting the top border option, while those of cells A6 to E6 and A16 to E16 were entered using the bottom border option.

Using Functions

All Spreadsheet programs have inbuilt functions which can be used to carry out various calculations using information held in rows or columns.

To illustrate how the summation function can be used, make cell E5 the active cell, and type:

=Sum(

then use the mouse pointer to highlight the cells in the summation range (B5 to D5 in this case). What appears against the cell indicator is the entry

Sum(B5:D5

which has to be completed by typing the closing parenthesis (round bracket) and pressing the **Enter** key.

Note: As soon as you type =S in a cell, all the available functions starting with that letter appear in a drop-down menu, as shown in Fig. 9.14. Typing another letter produces a list of functions starting with that letter.

=S
SERIESSUM(x, n, m, coefficients)
SIGN(number)
SIN(number)
SINH(number)
SQRT(number)
SQRTPI(number)
SUM(number_1, number_2, ... number_30)
SUMIF(range, criteria, sum_range)
SUMPRODUCT(array 1, array 2, ... array 30)
SUMSQ(number_1, number_2, ... number_30)

Fig. 9.14 Functions Starting with Letter S

To see a list of all available functions, with an explanation on what they do and how they can be used, click the **Help** button and type 'Functions' in the **What can we help you with?** box. Then follow the link **Functions – Functions** and click on **Static version of this document**. A list of functions, far too numerous for us to include in this book (the list is also copyright), are categorised under the following headings:

Array, Date, Filter, Financial, Google, Info, Logical, Lookup, Math, Operator, Statistical, and Text.

The list can be printed on paper for future use, which we strongly suggest you do, as this is an alternative list from the one that is displayed by the program itself – more about this shortly.

The Formulas Tab Sheet

Another clever feature of the Google Spreadsheet program is the facility to automatically enter the above =Sum() function (and several others) into the worksheet. First click the **Formulas** tab of the Menu bar and look at the changed Toolbar options, shown in Fig. 9.15 below.

Fig. 9.15 The Formulas Toolbar

Several links to commonly used functions are listed in the Toolbar, such as **Sum**, **Count**, **Average**, etc. There is also a link to **more**, which when clicked lists all the functions under the categories discussed earlier. In what follows we will show you how to use the **Sum** link in our example.

To automatically summate a series of numbers in either a column or a row, place the active cell below the column, or to the right of the row, and click the **Sum** link on the **Formulas** Toolbar. What is now displayed in the active cell is:

=Sum(

As an example, we will use this method to sum the contents of range B8:D8. So the active cell here will be E8 in which the characters =Sum(will be displayed when **Sum** is clicked.

Next, to enter the arguments of the function, either type the range B8:D8, or use the mouse to highlight the range by clicking on cell B8 and while holding the left mouse button down move the mouse pointer to cell D8 (see Fig. 9.16).

Fig. 9.16 Building up the Sum Function

Note: The range B8:D8 is shaded because it was selected by us with the mouse. **With functions, you cannot use the keyboard to highlight a range**.

Cell E8 is the cell we want the result of the summation to appear in. The label above this cell is inserted automatically by the Spreadsheet, while below it, it displays the type of function arguments it expects.

With both methods you need to type the closing parenthesis ')', and press **Enter** to complete the operation. It might be a few seconds before the result of the calculation is displayed on your screen, because the Spreadsheet has to be updated on the server where it is being held – you'll see the word "Updating" appear in red on the left of your screen.

Defining Range Names

We mentioned above two ways of defining a range of cells: by typing the range, or highlighting it using the mouse. There is a third way which uses 'range names'. For example, cell range B8:D8 refers to 'Wages', so we could use the **Range names** Toolbar button on the **Formulas** tab sheet to define the range and use 'Wages' as the function argument.

To define a cell range by a name, select the cell range with the mouse (say B8:D8) then click the **Range name** Toolbar button on the **Formulas** tab sheet and select **Define new** from the drop-down menu. This opens the window shown in Fig. 9.17, in which the cell range is already entered. All we have to do is give this range the name 'Wages' in the **Nickname** box and click **Save**.

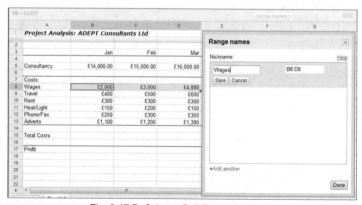

Fig. 9.17 Defining a Cell Range by Name

To use a range name as the argument to a function (in our example 'Wages'), make cell E8 the active cell, click the **Sum** link, and when the function =Sum(appears in the cell, click the **Range name** button and select **Wages** from the drop-down menu (see Fig. 9.18), where both the action that has to be taken and the result of that action are displayed.

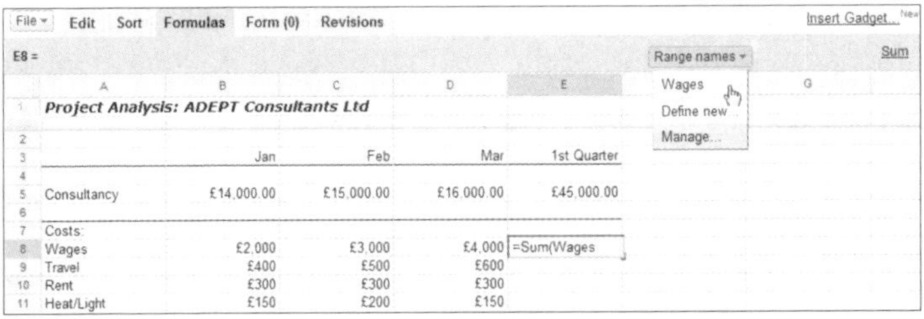

File ▾	Edit	Sort	**Formulas**	Form (0)	Revisions		Insert Gadget...	
E8 =						Range names ▾		Sum
	A	B	C	D	E	Wages	G	
1	*Project Analysis: ADEPT Consultants Ltd*					Define new		
2						Manage...		
3			Jan	Feb	Mar	1st Quarter		
4								
5	Consultancy	£14,000.00	£15,000.00	£16,000.00	£45,000.00			
6								
7	Costs:							
8	Wages	£2,000	£3,000	£4,000	=Sum(Wages			
9	Travel	£400	£500	£600				
10	Rent	£300	£300	£300				
11	Heat/Light	£150	£200	£150				

Fig. 9.18 Using a Range by Name in a Function

Copying Cell Contents

To copy information, such as the Sum() function, into other cells, select the cell (say E5) and copy it using the **Copy** icon on the **Edit** tab sheet (or the **Ctrl+C** key combination), point to the cell (or range of cells) you would like to copy it into (say E8:E13) and click the **Paste** icon (or use the **Ctrl+V** key combination). Immediately this is done, the actual sums of the 'relative' columns appear in the target area.

Notice that when you activate cell E5, the function target range is B5:D5, while when you activate cell E8 the function target range changes to B8:D8 which indicates that copying formulae with this method causes the 'relative' target range to be copied. Had the 'absolute' target range been copied instead, the result of the various summations would have been wrong. Also note that the formatting of cell E5 was also copied to the target area.

Note: The above method of copying formulas in cells will not work had you copied cells containing **Range names**, as these, by definition, refer to an 'absolute' target range.

Next, complete the insertion of functions and formulas in the rest of the worksheet, noting that 'Total Costs' is the summation of rows 8 through 13, 'Profit' is the subtraction of 'Total Costs' from 'Consultancy', and that 'Cumulative' in row 19 refers to cumulative profit.

Finally, add another column to your worksheet to calculate (and place in column F) the average monthly values of earnings, costs, and profit, using the =Avg( ) function which can also be obtained by clicking the **Average** link on the **Formulas** Toolbar.

The worksheet, up to this point, should look like the one in Fig. 9.19 below, in which we have also emboldened all the column and row titles. You will also need to use the **Format** Toolbar option on the **Edit** tab sheet to format some of the cells to what is shown here.

Note: As mentioned previously, be patient whenever you make a change to your worksheet. Sometimes the 'Updating' warning does not kick in quickly enough and you might think that nothing is happening! Remember, you are changing your work on the Google site which has to be alerted!

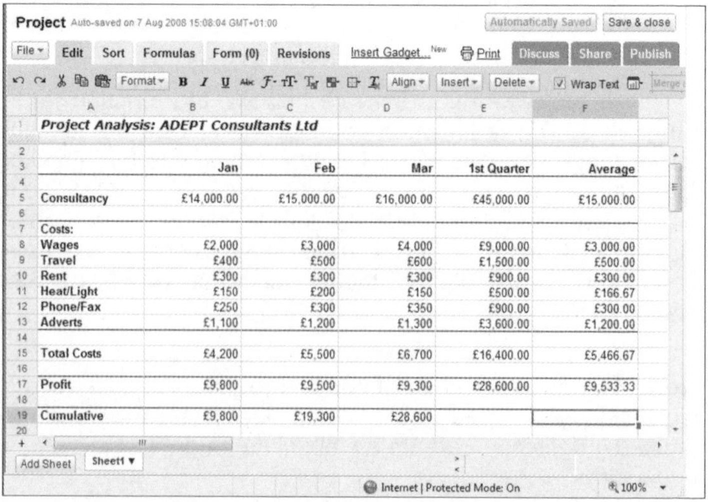

Fig. 9.19 The Completed First Quarter Worksheet of Adept Consultants.

Erasing Cell Contents

If you make any mistakes and copy information into cells you did not mean to, then choose the **Delete** Toolbar button on the **Edit** tab sheet. To blank the contents within a range of adjacent cells, first select the cell block, then click the button.

There are also the **Undo** and **Redo** Toolbar options on the **Edit** tab sheet which take you one step back (or forward) from your current editing position.

Printing a Worksheet

To print a worksheet, click on the **Print** link, shown here to the left, to open the **Print Settings** window shown in Fig. 9.20 below.

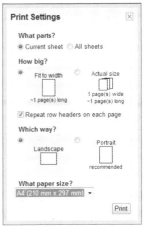

Fig. 9.20 The Print Settings Window

Note that the default print settings are **Current sheet**, **Fit to width**, **Repeat row headers on each page**, **Landscape**, and for size of paper, **Letter 8.5" x 11"**. If you are in the UK, change the size of the paper to **A4**.

Clicking the **Print** button creates a PDF file and sends it to Adobe Reader, which means you have the chance to preview your work before it is printed on paper.

What appears now on your screen is shown in Fig. 9.21 on the next page. To print it, click the **Print** icon on the Adobe Reader Toolbar.

If you do not have Adobe Reader on your computer, you can download a free version of it from the Adobe Web site at **www.adobe.com**.

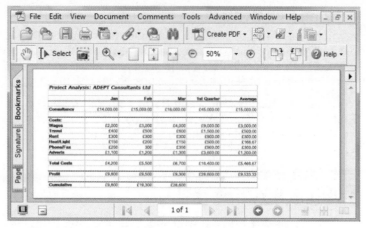

Fig. 9.21 Previewing a Worksheet in Adobe Reader

Controlling Cell Contents

We will now add some more information to the worksheet with the insertion of another quarter's figures between columns E and F. In fact, we need to insert four columns altogether.

In general, you can insert or delete columns and rows in a worksheet, copy cell contents (including formulae) from one part of the worksheet to another and freeze titles in order to make entries into cells easier. In what follows we discuss all these facilities.

Inserting Rows and Columns

To insert columns into a worksheet, point to the column heading where a column is to be inserted, in our case F, and press the left mouse button, which highlights the whole column. Then choose the **Insert**, **Insert Column Right** option on the **Edit** tab sheet, or right-click with the mouse and select **Insert 1 Right** from the displayed drop-down menu. Had you highlighted a specific cell, say F1, the **Insert** Toolbar button would have give you the option of inserting either columns, or rows.

Repeat the insertion command three more times so that the column headed 'Average' appears in column J. We can now copy everything from the first quarter to the second, thus copying all the formulas, then we would only need to edit the actual numeric information within the various columns and some labels.

Revisions

If, for any reason, you make a mess of your worksheet, click the **Revisions** tab, then use the **Older** or **Newer** buttons on the displayed tab sheet, to choose from saved and timed versions of your worksheet.

When you find the correct previous version of your work, as shown for us in Fig. 9.22, click the **Revert to this one** button pointed to below. You'll be asked to confirm your choice.

If you can't find what you are looking for and you want to exit the **Revisions** tab sheet, click any other tab on the Menu Toolbar. What displays on your screen then, is the worksheet you were working on prior to clicking the **Revert to this one** button.

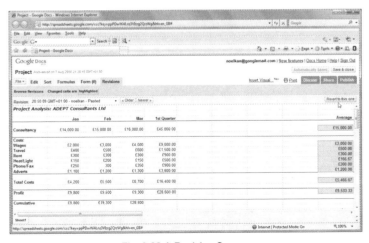

Fig. 9.22 A Revision Screen

Freezing Labels

By the time the highlighted bar is moved to column J, the 'labels' in column A have scrolled to the left and are outside the viewing area of the screen. This will make editing of numeric information very difficult if we can't see what refers to what. Therefore, before we attempt any further editing, it would be a good idea to use the **Sort** tab sheet to freeze the labels in column A and rows 1 to 3.

Note: In this Spreadsheet you cannot freeze a column which is part of a merged column, as is the case in our example with the Project Analysis title in cell A1. Therefore, before you continue, select the merged cell of the title and in the **Edit** tab sheet click the **Break apart** button pointed to in Fig. 9.23. Once this is done, press the **Delete** key on the keyboard to delete the contents of the resulting cell.

Fig. 9.23 Breaking Apart Merged Cells

Now, use the **Sort** tab sheet to freeze 3 rows and 1 column using the buttons shown in Fig. 9.24. To unfreeze rows or columns use the respective **No frozen** option.

File ▼	Edit	Sort	Formulas	Form (0)	Revisions	
Sort sheet by Column A		A -> Z Z -> A		Freeze header rows ▼	Freeze columns ▼	
	A	B	C	No frozen headers		E
1				Freeze **1** row		
2				Freeze **2** rows		
3		Jan		Freeze **3** rows	Mar	1st Quarter
4				Freeze **4** rows		
5	Consultancy	£14,000.00	£15,(	Freeze **5** rows	0.00	£45,000.00
6						
7	Costs:					

Fig. 9.24 Freezing Header Rows and Columns

On carrying out the above suggestions, the labels on the first 3 rows and column 1 are frozen, but the highlighter can still be moved into the frozen area.

Now, moving around the worksheet leaves the labels in these rows and column frozen on the screen. Carry this out and change the numbers in the worksheet cells F5 to H13 to those in Fig. 9.25 below.

	A	F	G	H	I	J
1						
2						
3		April	May	Jun	2nd Quarter	Average
4						
5	Consultancy	£15,500.00	£16,000.00	£16,500.00	£48,000.00	£15,000.00
6						
7	Costs:					
8	Wages	£3,500	£4,000	£4,500	£12,000.00	£3,000.00
9	Travel	£500	£550	£580	£1,630.00	£500.00
10	Rent	£300	£300	£300	£900.00	£300.00
11	Heat/Light	£150	£120	£100	£370.00	£166.67
12	Phone/Fax	£300	350	£400	£1,050.00	£300.00
13	Adverts	£1,250	£1,300	£1,350	£3,900.00	£1,200.00
14						
15	Total Costs	£6,000.00	£6,620.00	£7,230.00	£19,850.00	£5,466.67
16						
17	Profit	£9,500	£9,380	£9,270	£28,150.00	£9,533.33
18						
19	Cumulative	£9,500	£18,880	£28,150		

Fig. 9.25 Worksheet Displaying Information on Second Quarter

Note: If you examine this worksheet carefully, you will notice that two errors have occurred; one of these has to do with the average calculations in column J, while the other has to do with the accumulated values in the second quarter.

Non-contiguous Address Range

The calculations of average values in column J of the above worksheet are wrong because the range values in the formula are still those entered for the first quarter only.

To correct these, double-click cell J5 and edit the formula displayed in the cell from =Avg(B5:D5) to

```
=Avg(B5:D5,F5:H5)
```

which on pressing **Enter** changes the value shown in cell J5. To exit the edit mode, press **Esc**. Finally, replicate the formula to the J8:J13 cell range.

Relative and Absolute Cell Addresses

To see the effect of relative versus absolute addressing, type in cell E19 the formula =E5–E15, which will be interpreted as relative addressing. Now, copying the formula in cell E19 to cell E21 to calculate the 'Profit/Quart', gives the wrong (negative) answer because the cell references in the copied formula are now given as =E7–E17, as the references were copied relatively.

To obtain the correct answer we need to change the formula in E19 by editing it to =E5-E15, which is interpreted as absolute addressing. Copying this formula into cell E21 calculates the correct result.

The $ sign must prefix both the column reference and the row reference. Mixed cell addressing is permitted; as for example when a column address reference is needed to be taken as absolute, while a row address reference is needed to be taken as relative. In such a case, only the column letter is prefixed by the $ sign.

Finally, correct the formulas for the Cumulative cells to obtain the results shown in Fig. 9.26.

	1st Quarter	April	May	Jun	2nd Quarter	Average
5 Consultancy	£45,000.00	£15,500.00	£16,000.00	£16,500.00	£48,000.00	£15,500.00
6						
7 Costs:						
8 Wages	£9,000.00	£3,500	£4,000	£4,500	£12,000.00	£3,500.00
9 Travel	£1,500.00	£500	£550	£580	£1,630.00	£521.67
10 Rent	£900.00	£300	£300	£300	£900.00	£300.00
11 Heat/Light	£500.00	£150	£120	£100	£370.00	£145.00
12 Phone/Fax	£900.00	£300	350	£400	£1,050.00	£325.00
13 Adverts	£3,600.00	£1,250	£1,300	£1,350	£3,900.00	£1,250.00
14						
15 Total Costs	£16,400.00	£6,000.00	£6,620.00	£7,230.00	£19,850.00	£6,041.67
16						
17 Profit	£28,600.00	£9,500	£9,380	£9,270	£28,150.00	£9,458.33
18						
19 Cumulative	£28,600.00	£38,100	£47,480	£56,750	£56,750.00	
20						
21 Profit/Quarter	£28,600.00				£28,150.00	

Fig. 9.26 Demonstrating Relative and Absolute Cell Addressing.

 To improve the looks of this worksheet, we could use the **Background colour** button on the **Edit** tab sheet, shown here, to colour parts of the worksheet. See if you can emulate what is shown in **G31**.

Adding Spreadsheet Charts

Google's Spreadsheet allows you to represent information in graphical form which makes data more accessible to non-expert users who might not be familiar with the spreadsheet format.

To use the charting facility, first select the data range to be charted on your worksheet, such as A8:D13 (for the first quarter) on our file **Project**, and then click the **Add** button on the **Edit** tab sheet and **select Chart** as shown here This opens the **Create chart** window, shown in Fig. 9.27.

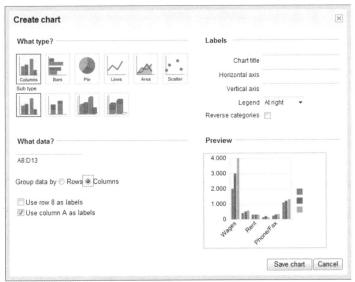

Fig. 9.27 The Create Chart Screen

As you click the icons in the **What type?** section, an example of each, based on the selected worksheet data, is shown in the **Preview** box. Although the program has six main two-dimensional chart types, each one of these has several subtypes, some in three dimensions. Further, there are many optional ways to view each type (grouped by Rows or Columns), which allows you to add considerably to the list.

To enhance your charts you can add titles, legends, and labels. These charts (you can have several per Spreadsheet) can be displayed on the screen and can be sent to an appropriate output device, such as a printer.

The main chart types available are listed next, with their **Charting** Toolbar icons. These chart types are normally used for the following relationships between data:

Column

For comparing separate items (noncontinuous data which are related over time) by depicting changes in vertical columns; with 2-D or 3-D options. The stacked options show relationships to the whole.

Bar

For comparing differences in data (noncontinuous data that are not related over time) by depicting changes in horizontal bars to show positive and negative variations from a given position.

Pie

For comparing parts with the whole. Displays data blocks as slices of a pie. Can contain only one series; 2-D or 3-D options available.

Line

For representing data values with points joined by lines and appearing at equal intervals along the x-axis. For such charts, the x-axis could be intervals in time, such as labels representing months.

Area

For showing a volume relationship between two series, such as production or sales, over time.

Scatter

For showing the relationship, or degree of relationship, between numeric values in different groups of data; used for finding patterns or trends in data.

Charts can be displayed on the screen at the same time as the worksheet, but in a separate window. As charts are dynamic, any changes made to the data are automatically reflected on the defined charts.

In Fig. 9.27 we used the data within the range of A8:D13 for displaying a Column chart. The reason why we did not use a data range covering the six-month period is because the specified range of data to be charted should be contiguous. Therefore we have two choices; either we copy the data for the six-month period to a new sheet, or we delete the columns E and I (the totals for each quarter) from our example.

For this example we choose to copy the data for the two three-monthly periods into a contiguous area on another sheet. So, first click the **Add Sheet** button at the bottom of the worksheet, shown in Fig. 9.28, to create **Sheet2**, then click the down-arrow against it to display the menu associated with this sheet. We suggest you **Rename** this sheet to **Six-monthly Data**, then use the **Move left** option to move the worksheet in front of **Sheet1**, then rename **Sheet1** to **Original Data**.

Fig. 9.28 Adding a Work Sheet

Next, select and copy the cell block A1:D18, then click on the tab of the **Six-monthly Data** sheet to make it the current sheet and click the **Edit**, **Paste** button on the **Edit** tab sheet, shown here to the left.

When you use the **Paste** button on the **Edit** tab sheet, a menu of options is displayed, as shown here. The **Paste** option pastes all formulas.

The **Paste values only** option pastes the results appearing on cells, but not their underlining formulas, while the **Paste format only** option, is only used to copy the formatting of another cell, not the whole sheet.

Finally, copy the contents of cell range F1:J18, then use the **Delete** button on the **Edit** tab sheet to delete column I, which is the one with the Totals for the second three-monthly period.

To move the heading **Project Analysis** to a more central position (if you have inserted it again), you will have to **Break apart** the cells containing the title, before doing so. The resultant sheet should look as shown in Fig. 9.29.

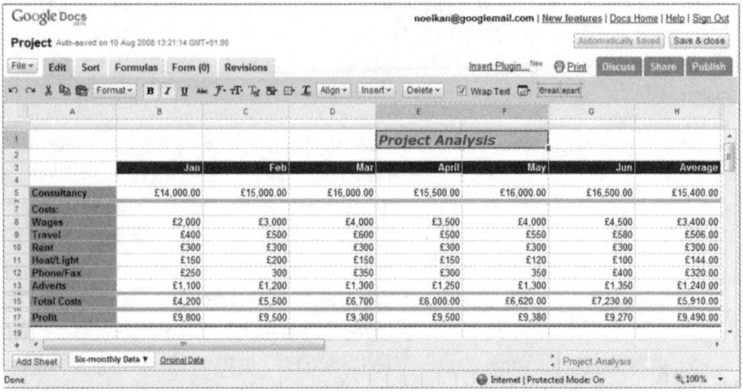

Project Analysis

	Jan	Feb	Mar	April	May	Jun	Average
Consultancy	£14,000.00	£15,000.00	£16,000.00	£15,500.00	£16,000.00	£16,500.00	£15,400.00
Costs:							
Wages	£2,000	£3,000	£4,000	£3,500	£4,000	£4,500	£3,400.00
Travel	£400	£500	£600	£500	£550	£580	£506.00
Rent	£300	£300	£300	£300	£300	£300	£300.00
Heat/Light	£150	£200	£150	£150	£120	£100	£144.00
Phone/Fax	£250	300	£350	£300	350	£400	£320.00
Adverts	£1,100	£1,200	£1,300	£1,250	£1,300	£1,350	£1,240.00
Total Costs	£4,200	£5,500	£6,700	£6,000.00	£6,620.00	£7,230.00	£5,910.00
Profit	£9,800	£9,500	£9,300	£9,500	£9,380	£9,270	£9,490.00

Fig. 9.29 The Contiguous Six-monthly Data

Do check that the actual values displayed are what they should be. By now you should have spotted the fact that what is displayed under 'Average' is wrong, because the cell ranges of the underlying formulae were copied wrongly. This happened as a result of the way we copied the various columns across from one sheet to the other.

Creating Charts

To obtain a chart of 'Income' versus 'Months', block cell range A3:G5 and click the **Insert** button on the **Edit** tab sheet and select **Chart**. On the displayed **Create chart** window (see Fig. 9.27), accept the default selection of a **Column** chart and provide a 'Chart title' and **Labels** for the Horizontal and Vertical axes. Click the **Save chart** button at the bottom of the window to display the screen shown in Fig. 9.30.

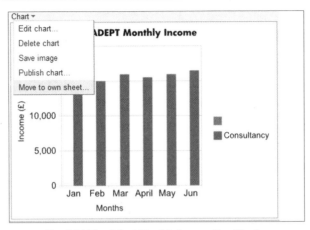

Fig. 9.30 The Adept Monthly Income Bar Chart.

Clicking a chart displays a drop-down menu with options to edit, delete, save as an image, publish, or move a chart to its own sheet. We choose the last option which also allows us to gain access to the worksheet for further work. The Spreadsheet now displays the chart on a new sheet giving it the name **Chart1**. Rename this to **Income Chart**.

To select a different type chart, but with the same cell range selection as before, click on the **Edit chart** button on the sheet displaying your chart, which displays the **Create chart** window for you to make a different chart selection. If, on the other hand, you want to chart a different cell range, then you must return to the worksheet and redefine the new cell range for a chart of your choice.

Stacked Costs Chart

On the next page, we show in Fig. 9.31 the required preparation for creating a **Stacked Costs** chart with actual 'Months' appearing on the vertical axis. To achieve this we need to copy the cell range B3:G3 to cell range B7:G7, so that when we block the cell range A7:G13 we include all the contiguous information required for labelling the chart correctly, including the months range.

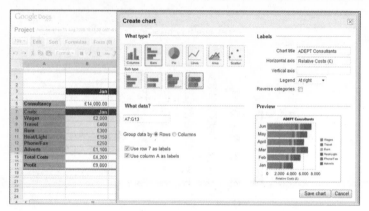

Fig. 9.31 A Stacked Costs Chart

This type of chart is not very distinctive in black and white, so have a look at the finished chart in **G32** in Colour Gallery 2.

Drawing a Pie Chart

As an additional example in chart drawing, we will use the 'Average' values of the costs from the worksheet **Six-monthly Data** to plot a pie chart.

However, since the information required for drawing a Pie chart is at either end of the worksheet, we need to copy range A8:A13 to A20:A25 and range H8:H13 to B20:B25.

Next, select the copied information in cell range A20:B25 (which is now contiguous), and click the **Insert** button on the **Edit** tab sheet, select **Chart**, and choose the 3-D Pie chart type. The resulting colourful Pie chart is shown in **G33**.

* * *

You can do a lot more with Google's Spreadsheet, but we do not propose to introduce more here. After going through the example in this chapter, you should be able to do most things by yourself.

10

Presentations and Calendars

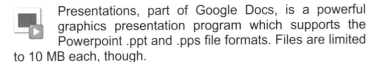 Presentations, part of Google Docs, is a powerful graphics presentation program which supports the Powerpoint .ppt and .pps file formats. Files are limited to 10 MB each, though.

If you intend to upload an existing Presentation, or to invite colleagues to either collaborate or view your work, we suggest you refer to the beginning of Chapter 8, as these subjects were covered there and are common to all Google Documents and to the Calendar.

Creating a Presentation

To create a Presentation from scratch, in Google **Documents**, click the **New** button and select **Presentation** from the drop-down menu, as shown in Fig. 10.1.

Fig. 10.1 Creating a New Presentation

When you first enter Google Presentation, the program displays the screen shown in Fig. 10.2 on the next page.

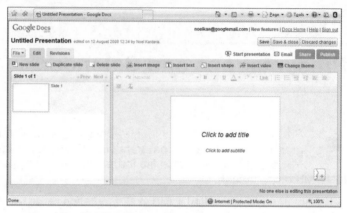

Fig. 10.2 The Opening Blank Presentation Screen

This is known as a 'Blank' presentation. However, if you don't like the idea of spending time designing your own presentation from scratch, it might be worth while having a look at the **From template** option in Fig. 10.1, as you might find a design that suits your purpose.

Selecting the latter option, displays a screen with templates for Documents, Spreadsheets, and Presentations. Fig. 10.3 shows some of the available presentation templates from which we will choose the one entitled 'Latitude'.

Fig. 10.3 Templates for Presentations

You can get a better appreciation of these templates if you see them in colour, as shown in **G34** in Colour Gallery 2.

The selected template has six slides and the suggested topics of each slide can be changed to suit your needs. So click the **Use this template** button, to display the screen shown in Fig. 10.4 below.

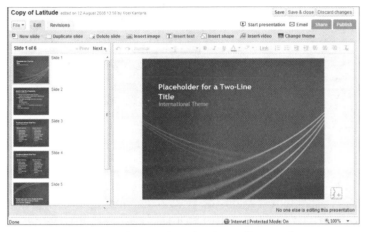

Fig. 10.4 The Selected Template for our Presentation

You can use the **File** menu, shown here in Fig. 10.5, to

Rename the presentation to a name of your choice (say **My Presentation**), **Print** a presentation with or without speaker notes, **Save** your work in different file formats, such as Adobe **PDF**, PowerPoint **PPT**, or simple **Text**, use the **Start presentation** option to see a slide show of your work, etc.

Clicking within the text area of a slide, activates the formatting Toolbar, as shown in Fig. 10.6 on the next page.

Fig. 10.5 Renaming a Presentation

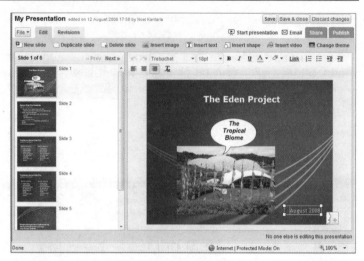

Fig. 10.6 Editing a Template

As you can see, all the text editing tools are available to you, with options for changing the font type and size, enhancing text, aligning text within the text boxes, and repositioning it on the slide. We used all these tools to change the title of the first slide of the template to what is shown above. When you click on another slide, it is enlarged in the working area so you can work on its text.

Note that the **Edit** tab Menu bar contains options for adding and deleting slides, inserting images (provided they are less than 2 MB), text, shapes and video. Above, we have inserted a picture and used a shape to annotate it. You can see it in colour in **G35**.

You can even change the theme of your work. If, after changing the theme of your presentation you do not like what you see, click the **Discard changes** button at the top right of the screen to revert to the previous theme.

Speaker notes can be produced by clicking the icon shown here to the left, which displays at the bottom of the working area of your presentation.

We leave it to you to try these and other aspects of Google Presentations. They should be self-explanatory.

Google Calendar

 Google Calendar is a free Web-based calendar application that enables you to keep track of all your important events and appointments online. It works in a Web browser (such as Google Chrome, Microsoft Internet Explorer 6.0+ or Firefox 1.07+), in which both JavaScript and cookies must be enabled. Then no matter where you are, once you are online, you will have access to your calendar.

To import an existing calendar, or create one from scratch, you need to start Google in your browser and click on **Calendar**. This opens the 'Sign in' window, and then displays the screen shown in Fig. 10.7, for you to enter your name, location, and time zone. Then click on **Continue**.

Fig. 10.7 The Sign up Screen for Google Calendar

Customising a Calendar

To customise a calendar, click the **Settings** link at the top right of the screen and provide your preferences regarding language, date format, default view, etc., on the displayed screen. To apply these preferences to your Calendar, scroll down the bottom of the window and click the **Save** button.

What displays on your screen now should be similar (depending on your preferences) to that shown in Fig. 10.8 on the next page, where we show a monthly view.

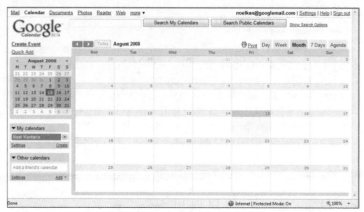
Fig. 10.8 The Customised Calendar Screen

Importing a Calendar

Before you can import an existing calendar, start the program which holds your calendar (in our case Microsoft Outlook) and export it to a Comma Separated Values (.CSV) file in Windows. With Outlook you use the **File**, **Import and Export** command.

Note: At some point, the program asks you to specify the starting and ending dates for the export procedure. As the Google Calendar does not support the import of more than a year's information at a time, you might find it necessary to slice your calendar intro several one-year slots.

Finally, save the exported file somewhere you can find it later.

To import the calendar into Google, click the down-arrow

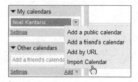

against the **Add** option of **Other Calendars**, and select the **Import Calendar** option from the drop-down menu shown in Fig. 10.9.

Fig. 10.9 Importing a Calendar

The screen that opens next, allows you to browse and find your saved calendar. Having located your exported .CSV file, click the **Import** button to display information on the number of imported events.

You can also use the drop-down menu shown in Fig. 10.5, to add other public calendars, such as public holidays, etc., as shown in Fig. 10.10 below.

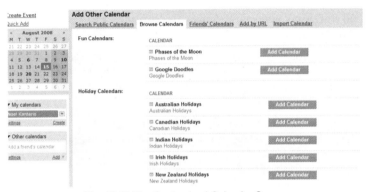

Fig. 10.10 The Customised Calendar Screen

Events added by **Other Calendars** only show in your own calendar if they are highlighted in the **Other Calendars** area. Such events can be switched on/off (highlighted/dimmed) by clicking their entry in the **Other Calendars** list.

Calendar Colours

The default colour for all calendar entries, is red. This can be confusing when trying to merge two calendars.

To choose a different colour for one of the calendars, click the down-arrow against it and select from the displayed menu in Fig. 10.11.

Fig. 10.11 Selecting Event Colour

To see Fig. 10.11 in colour, refer to **G36** where we show events from our calendar in red and those of the imported UK Holidays Calendar in green.

Copying Events from Other Calendars

Having changed the colour of events of a calendar in the **Other Calendars** list, it is easy to distinguish between the two and copy events from one into the other. To do so, click an imported event and select the **copy to my calendar** link that displays.

You should be selective in what you copy in your calendar. For example, the UK Public Holidays Calendar includes all public holidays in all the regions of the UK, which might not be what you want.

In the example shown in Fig. 10.12, we show the screen that displayed when an event was being copied to our calendar. Note that, by default, the event does not repeat, but you have the ability to change it.

Fig. 10.12 Changing a Copied Event

After copying what you want from the inserted calendar, make it inactive or even delete it by clicking **Settings** and deleting it on the displayed **Calendar Settings** window.

Editing Calendar Entries

Since Google Calendar only imports a year's information, repeated items within that year loose their repeat status. Therefore, to repeat items such as regular meetings, birthdays or anniversaries, including entries from additional calendars, you need to edit them manually.

Clicking on such an event, gives you two options; **Delete**, or **Edit event details**. Selecting the latter, opens a window similar to that shown in Fig. 10.11. Note that for birthdays and anniversaries, you might want to be informed a couple of days prior to the event, which can be requested under the **Reminder** area of the displayed window.

You might think that all this involves an awful lot of time, but you only need to do it once, and having done it for one entry, changing the remaining ones becomes progressively easier.

To add a new event, click on a calendar day, give the event a title on the displayed screen, then click **Create Event**, and type the information.

Fig. 10.13 Adding a Calendar Event

Sharing a Calendar

From the menu in Fig. 10.11, you can also choose the **Share this calendar** option, which opens the window in Fig. 10.14.

Fig. 10.14 Sharing a Calendar with Others

It might be a good idea, however, to create an additional calendar for sharing with colleagues, rather that sharing your own personal calendar. This can be done by using the **Settings** option under **My calendar**.

Searching Calendars

You can search for items or events in either your own calendars or in Public calendars. To do so, type a query in the text box provided at the top of the calendar screen and click the appropriate button (see Fig. 10.14 on the previous page).

To see the type of expected queries, click the **Show Search Options** link next to the search buttons, to open the screen shown in Fig. 10.15 below.

Fig. 10.15 Calendar Search Options

* * *

Google's Calendar has additional features which we are sure you will be able to explore by yourself, having given you sufficient information on how to use it. Good luck!

* * *

11

Google Photos

Google Photos has two main programs to use for viewing and handling photographs. You can organise and edit your photos on your computer using **Picasa**, and store and display them online with **Picasa Web Albums**.

To work with videos, Google has **YouTube**, the free service that allows anyone to view and share videos online.

Picasa for your Photographs

Picasa is a free downloadable program from Google that helps you find, edit and share all the pictures on your computer. Each time Picasa is opened, it automatically locates any new pictures and sorts them into 'folders'. It also has very powerful tools for editing your photos, almost making that expensive graphics program redundant. Picasa Web Albums lets you download and store your photos online, making them easy to share with the rest of the World. For a free program, it really has a lot to offer.

To use Picasa your computer needs to run under Windows XP or Vista and have at least 256MB of RAM and 100MB of available hard disc space. Most do these days.

Two days before starting this chapter Google not only released the new Chrome Web browser, but also released Picasa 3, the new version that we have used here. It really is a great program and deserves a book on its own.

To get Picasa, go to **http://picasa.google.com** which opens the screen shown in Fig. 11.1 on the next page. When you have viewed the video and read about Picasa 3's new features, press the **Download..** button to start the process.

Fig. 11.1 The Picasa Home Page

As the download proceeds, read the License Agreement and click **I Agree**, accept the destination folder suggested for the 24.5MB download (or **Browse** to another location), and click **Install**.

Once the program is installed, the box shown in Fig. 11.2 is opened. We suggest you select for a limited scan of your PC, as shown here, or you may be surprised at the results. You can always add more locations later.

Fig. 11.2 Giving Scan Instructions

If you let Picasa scan your entire computer, it will find cached Internet files, graphics from computer programs, and other images that you probably don't need in your photo album. You can remove files later, but it's much easier not to import them in the first place.

When the box shown in **G37**, in Colour Gallery 2, opens we suggest you choose to use Picasa 3's superb new Photo Viewer to preview photos from Windows folders. It really is the best we have seen. More about this later.

The Picasa Window

When Picasa opens for the first time you will see that it has listed all of your photos by date and has retained the same file structure as your hard drive, as shown for us in Fig. 11.3.

Fig. 11.3 Picasa's Opening View on our Computer

To understand Picasa it is important to remember that the program scans your computer for photos, and displays them for you. It does not keep, copy, or store, your photos, they are always maintained in their original files on your hard disc. But it does keep and process references to them which it stores in its own database. **If you delete a photo from a folder in Picasa, the photo will be deleted from the folder on your computer.** So beware.

On the left of the Picasa window (Fig. 11.3) is a Folders List pane, with the main working area, or library, to the right displaying thumbnails of the images in the selected folder. Although the thumbnails are grouped by the folders on your hard disc, you can continuously scroll through thumbnails of all of your photos, using the scroll bar on the extreme right (shown here) or by rolling your mouse wheel. So in the working area you can access any photo on your computer without having to physically open its folder.

The scroll bar is a little unusual and needs some comment. If you are looking in the middle of a folder, clicking the ⊼ icon moves you to the top of the folder. Clicking it again moves you up to the top of the next folder. Clicking the ⊻ icon moves you down to the top of the next folder below. Clicking the ⌃ and ⌄ icons move you up or down one row of thumbnails. You can also drag the central slider to move the thumbnails up or down continuously. To move quickly through a large number of photos, locate the folder you want in the Folders List on the left and click it. All this sounds a little heavy, but it works well once you try it.

Although you can continuously scroll through your folders of thumbnails, you always know where you are in the list as a header bar is placed between the folders, like the one shown in Fig. 11.4 below, and in colour in **G38**.

Fig. 11.4 A Typical Picasa Folder header Bar

The buttons on the Header bar allow you to carry out actions on the photos in the folder. We will look at these later on.

Changing Thumbnail Size

The easiest way to change the size of thumbnails in Picasa is to drag the Thumbnail Slider located below them and shown in Fig. 11.5. You can also use the **View**, **Small Thumbnails**, or **View**, **Normal Thumbnails** menu options, or the **Ctrl+1** and **Ctrl+2** keyboard shortcuts.

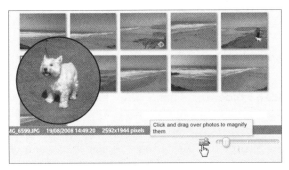

Fig. 11.5 The Loupe Tool and Thumbnail Slider

To look at the detail in your photos when browsing your library, click and drag the **Loupe** tool next to the slider. A round magnifying glass appears as shown in Fig. 11.5. As soon as you release the mouse button it will disappear.

You can also view a photo full size while working with thumbnails. Just select, or move the pointer over, a thumbnail and hold down the **Ctrl+Alt** keys together. Releasing the keys returns you to where you were.

Folders and Albums

As we have seen, the Folders List on the left of the Picasa window displays all your collections in Picasa. You may have noticed by now, though, that this does not just hold folders but 'Albums' as well. As shown in Fig. 11.6, your collections will normally include:

Albums   These are virtual folders that let you group related photos without moving your files around the disc. Albums only contain references to your picture files (which live in folders). They have green ▮* or ▮ blue icons.

Fig. 11.6

Folders   These contain files stored on your hard drive that have been scanned. They have a yellow 📁 folder icon.

Exported Pictures   These are folders of photos that you have exported from Picasa. 📁

Hidden Folders   These are folders that you have hidden, so that no one else can access them. 📁

Other Stuff   This has Folders containing videos or small image files (less than 250 x 250 pixels), or unusual image files. 📁

Folder Hierarchy

You can change the view of the Folders List with the **View**, **Folder View** menu command, and selecting from the **Flat Folder View**, **Tree View**, or **Simplified Tree View** options. The first two of these are also available with the 📇 📇 toggle button at the top of the Folders List. Examples of these two are shown in colour in **G39** and **G40**.

Flat Folder View is the default view and displays all the 'watched' and 'scan once' folders on your computer.

Tree View is a hierarchical view of all the 'watched' folders on your computer.

Simplified Tree View is a semi-hierarchical view of the folders which contain most of your photos, which may not actually reflect the folder structure of your disc.

Organising Your Photos

How you organise your photographs is obviously a personal choice. Some people just put them all into one folder and use Picasa to separate them into logical groupings or albums. We prefer to create a new dated folder for every batch of photos we download from our camera, then it is easy to sort the folders in date order in Windows.

You can move thumbnails by simply dragging them from folder to folder in Picasa, and it will confirm and move the corresponding files on your hard drive. This makes it very easy to organise your photo albums. If you want to drag an entire folder into another folder first select it with the **Ctrl+A** keyboard shortcut.

To permanently delete a photo from your computer using Picasa, just right-click it in a library folder and select **Delete from Disk** from the context menu. Clicking **Yes** in the **Confirm Delete** box will send it to the Windows recycle bin. If you delete a photo from an Album, it just removes it from the album. The photo itself remains in its folder.

If you drag a photo from one folder to another folder within Picasa, the photo changes actual folders on the disc. If, on the other hand, you drag a photo from a folder to an album, the album references the photo and appears to have the photo in it. But its file still physically resides in its folder.

To remove duplicate pictures from your Folders or Albums, right click the image and select **Hide**. The photo should be instantly removed from Picasa, but not deleted from disc.

The Photo Tray

When a folder is first selected, all the photos in it are 'effectively' selected and a small thumbnail appears in the Photo Tray (at the

Fig. 11.7 The Photo Tray

bottom-left of the Picasa window) with the number of photos on it, as shown here in Fig. 11.7.

To select a single photo in the Picasa library, just click on it. To select multiple photos in the same folder, keep the **Ctrl**

Fig. 11.8 The Photo Tray

key depressed and click them. Their thumbnails will then appear in the Photo Tray, as shown in Fig. 11.8. It displays the photos you currently have selected.

When you want to select photos from multiple folders or albums, you have to click the **Hold** button ✦ to anchor the thumbnails in the Photo Tray before moving to another folder. A green marker ◉ is placed on held thumbnails. Clicking the **Clear** button ○ will remove selected photos from the Photo Tray. The **Add To** button ▬▾ lets you add the selection from the Photo Tray to an existing or new Album.

Tags and Stars

Rather than physically moving all your photos, you can give them 'tags' or 'stars', and search for photos with these attributes when you want them. You could tag all the photos of friends and family with their names for instance. In Picasa 3 you can now add multi-word tags to your photos and they are stored in the actual photo files themselves.

To add a tag, select your photo and click the **Tag** button ▣ in the button

bar next to the Photo Tray area shown here, or use the **Ctrl+T** keyboard shortcut. The blue status bar at the bottom of the screen shows any tags that have been applied to your picture.

Fig. 11.9 Setting a Tag

Type the tag in the **Add Tag** box and click the **Add** button, as shown in Fig. 11.9. When you are finished, clicking the **Done** button will add the tags to the photo file.

In Picasa you can mark special photos in your collections with 'stars'. They are then automatically added to the **Starred Photos** Album for you to process as you want. To do this, just select the photo and click the **Star** button. A small yellow star is placed on the thumbnail, as shown here. The **Star** button is a toggle button so to remove the star you just click it again.

Searching for Photos

It is no surprise that a program as powerful as Picasa 3 has some very good searching facilities built in. These are found on the toolbar above the photo library as shown in Fig. 11.10.

Fig. 11.10 The Photo Filter and Search Options in Picasa 3

This shows both the search and filter tools and the green info bar that appears underneath when you use them. You can search for text associated with your photos, including filenames, tags, captions, Folder names, Album names, Collection names and camera maker. You just type your search term in the ⌕ ⬚ Search Box.

As you type each letter, the search results instantly change, as shown in Fig. 11.11, and a new **Search results for...** Album is added to the top of the Folders List. To clear a search, press the **Esc** key, or click the red **Clear your search** button ◄⊠ in the Search Box, or click the **Back to View All** button shown in Fig. 11.10 above.

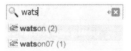

Fig. 11.11 Picasa
Search Results

You can filter your library photos by **date range** by moving the Slider shown in Fig. 11.10; to show only **starred photos** ★ , only **uploads to Web Albums** ⬆ , only **photos with faces** 👤 , or to show **movies only** ▣ .

Editing and Fixing Photos

When you double-click on a photo in the library, Picasa opens it in an editing window where you can fix common problems and create great effects in your photos. As shown in **G41** and **G42** there are three editing tabs filled with tools to help you improve your photos.

Basic Fixes   Buttons that work in one to two clicks to remove **Redeye**, **Crop**, **Auto colour**, **Auto contrast**, **Straighten**, **Fill light**, **Retouch** and add **Text** to your photos. Try the **I'm Feeling Lucky** button, it might just sort your photo out automatically.

Tuning   More advanced editing features with sliders to help you fix contrast and remove colour cast. Select from **Fill Light**, **Highlights**, **Shadows**, **Color Temperature**, and a **Neutral Color Picker**.

Effects   Effects are designed to help you turn a grey sky blue, brighten colours, and add photographic filters. There are 12 effects to choose from **Sharpen**, **Sepia**, **B&W**, **Warmify**, **Film Grain**, **Tint**, **Saturation**, **Soft Focus**, **Glow**, **Filtered B&W**, **Focal B&W**, and **Graduated Tint**.

At any stage you can cancel your editing with the **Undo Tuning** button. We think these tools are very good, especially for a free software program.

Details of any changes you make to a photo are saved in the Picasa database and a **.ini** file is also saved with the photo. The original photo file is not changed at all. As long as you use Picasa to handle your photos in the future this is fine.

If you click the `Save to Disk` button, Picasa saves any edits in the folder and overwrites the original photo files on disc, but it also creates a hidden sub-folder called **Originals** in the same folder and moves the original photos to it. So you should always have original copies of your photos to go back to.

Loading from Your Camera

With Picasa it is a doddle to transfer photos directly from your digital camera to your computer. If necessary, click Picasa's desktop icon to start the program, connect your camera to the computer (usually with a USB cable) and switch the camera to Playback Mode. Clicking the import button will start the procedure and open the Import tab shown in Fig. 11.12.

Fig. 11.12 Importing Photos from a Digital Camera

If you are lucky, your camera will be recognised as ours was above. If not, click the **Select Device** button and select it from a drop-down list. Then either click the **Import All** button, or select the photos you want to import and click on **Import Selected**. In our case the last 28 photos out of the 95 on the camera were selected.

In the **Finish Importing** box that opens next (Fig. 11.13) you control where the imported photos will be placed. To store them in an existing folder on your hard disc, leave **Enter a folder name for these photos** blank and click the **Browse** button to locate the folder you want. To put them in a new folder, type its name in the **Enter a folder name...** box.

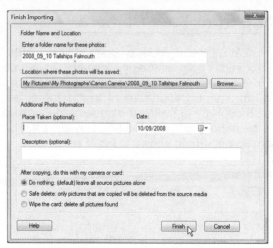

Fig. 11.13 The Finish Importing Dialogue Box

There are options to delete the original photos from your camera, but we prefer to do that manually and would recommend leaving the default **Do nothing...** option selected. Finally click the **Finish** button and the photos should be downloaded to your hard disc and appear in Picasa. This is by far the easiest way we have found so far.

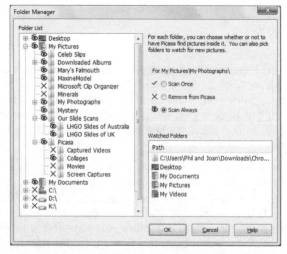

Fig. 11.14 Controlling Which Disc Folders Picasa Scans

If at any time you don't think Picasa is scanning a folder and is not keeping its contents up to date in the library, use the **Tools**, **Folder Manager** menu command and check the settings in the Folder Manager shown in Fig. 11.14. Watched folders should have the **Scan Always** mark ⊛ next to them. The **Scan Once** option gets Picasa to scan the folder, but not to look in it for updates in the future.

Using Your Photos

Once you have mastered Picasa and have all your photos organised the way you want, there is a large list of things you can actually do with them. These are most easily accessed with the buttons on one of the following two toolbars.

Fig. 11.15 The Library Toolbar

The tools in the small toolbar above the library pane (Fig. 11.15) act on all of the photos in the currently active Folder or Album.

Fig. 11.16 The Photo Tray Toolbar

To mix photos from different Folders and Albums, first place them in the Photo Tray and then use the tools in the bar to the right of the Photo Tray, shown in Fig. 11.16.

Playing a Slideshow

A slideshow is perhaps the first thing you'll want to do once you have your photos as and where you want them. Clicking the **Play** button will start one for the photos in the currently active Folder or Album.

You can control the show, once it has started, with the controls on the bar shown in Fig. 11.17 which appears on the screen when you move the mouse pointer.

Fig. 11.17 Controlling a Slideshow

Photo Collages

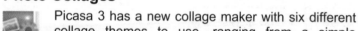 Picasa 3 has a new collage maker with six different collage themes to use, ranging from a simple **Contact Sheet**, as shown below, to a **Picture Pile** theme in which you can arrange, re-size and rotate your photos and choose the background.

Fig. 11.18 Creating a Photo Collage

You really must play with this tool; you can get some very good results.

Just clicking the **Desktop Background** button will make your photo collage into the Windows desktop wallpaper. You can also print, e-mail or upload them.

Movie Presentation

 In Picasa 3 you can take a collection of photos and videos and combine them into a movie, complete with soundtrack. You can easily add your own title slides and then post your creation to the Web with one click. We will leave it to you to find your way here, we just do not have the space.

Printing Photos

 You can select a photo or a range of photos and print them from Picasa by clicking the **Print** button. This opens the box shown in Fig. 11.19.

Fig. 11.19 Printing Photos from Picasa

You have many print options here, but we prefer to set the **Print Layout** to **Full Page** and click the **Printer Setup** button to control the printing layout from the printer software.

 If you click the **Shop** button on the Photo Tray toolbar, you can order prints of your photos online from a range of different printing services.

Sharing Your Photos

With the **Create Gift CD** button ⊕ , you can make a CD or DVD slide show of the photos in the current Folder or Album.

The **Geotag** button ⬤ gives you an easy way to embed location information within your photo files so that you can display them on Google Earth satellite maps for your friends to see. Longitude and latitude information is written to the photo's EXIF GPS metadata.

You can select photos and click the **Email** button ✉ to send them as attachments with a message. Picasa opens your default e-mail program to do this.

You can also post selected photos directly to your Blogger account by clicking the **BlogThis** button ⓑ.

The **Export** button 📁 lets you save copies of your edited photos. You can change the image size and quality or add a watermark to the exported photo.

Finally you can use the **Upload** button ⬆ to send the photos in the Photo Tray to a folder in your Picasa Web Albums space, also called Google Photos, provided by Google somewhere in the clouds.

Picasa Web Albums

With Google Photos, you organise and edit your photos on your computer using **Picasa**, and then you can store and display them online with **Picasa Web Albums**, which lets you upload and share your photos quickly and easily on the Web. Once you have registered, you get 1GB of free storage space for your photos, but if this is not enough, you can upgrade and pay for even more space.

The new **Sync to Web** button ⊂⬤⊃ in Picasa 3 lets you synchronise specific Folders or Albums on your computer to the Web. If you edit or add photos to these Folders or Albums on your computer, the changes will be automatically reflected in Picasa Web Albums online.

With Picasa's **Share** button ⟨ Share ⟩, you can invite your friends to share your Web Albums with just a click.

Uploading to Web Albums

To place your photos on the Web for all to see, open Picasa and select the photos that you want to 'publish'. To select multiple photos, press the **Ctrl** key while clicking the photos. Click the **Hold** button if you want to select from another Folder or Album. Your selected photos appear in the Photo Tray at the bottom-left of the Picasa window. When you have selected all the photos you want, click the **Upload to Web Album** button ☝. If you are not signed in to your Google Account, you should do this and, for the first time, provide information to set up your Web Album account. The **Upload to Web Albums** box then opens, as shown below.

Fig. 11.20 Uploading to Web Albums

Click the **New** button to create a new folder and fill in the **Album Title** and **Description** boxes. Make sure the **Public Album** radio button is selected, and click the **Upload** button. The Upload Manager will open and display the status of the upload. When the upload is complete, click the **View Online** button to launch the album in your browser. The result for us can be seen in colour in **G43**.

That's all there is to it. We will leave it to you to explore Web Albums further. We find it great fun, but don't let yourself become addicted!

You can open Web Albums at any time from Picasa by clicking the **Web Albums** link at the top of the window. If you don't want to work with Picasa, you can open it from the top of any Google page by clicking the **more**, **Photos** links.

Fig. 11.21 Name Tags Feature

Picasa Web Albums now includes a new **Name Tags** feature that can automatically group photos containing similar faces. This lets you rapidly tag many photos at once with the person's name.

Unfortunately when we wrote this it was not yet available outside the US.

Backing Up Your Photos

You can use your Web Albums space to backup your photos, but make sure you upload using the **Original size** option in the **Size to upload** drop-down list of the **Upload to Web Albums** box. This will use up your 1GB of space in about 300 average photos, so you may have to **Upgrade**.

Perhaps a better option, especially if you have an external hard disc, is to use Picasa's **Tools**, **Backup Pictures** menu command, click the **New Set** button and start a full backup of all your photos.

The Photo Viewer

When you install Picasa 3, the Picasa Photo Viewer is also installed, as shown in **G37**. This lets you to take a quick look at your images without having to use Picasa itself.

From your desktop or from within a Windows Explorer window, just double-clicking an image file will launch the Viewer, as shown in **G44**. The Viewer is usually opened with a full screen view but if you click outside the image boundary, the image will display in a window. If you double-click the image in the window it will display full screen again. Double-clicking again will zoom the photo. Rotating the scroll wheel on your mouse will step you through other photos in the same folder.

Fig. 11.22 The Photo Viewer Menu Bar

When you move the pointer to the bottom of the open image, a menu bar appears, as shown in Fig. 11.22 above. This shows a ribbon of thumbnails of the photos in the folder. Clicking one will jump the Viewer to that image. It also has buttons that let you zoom in and out, open Picasa 3 to edit the photo, start a slideshow, upload the photo to Web Albums, rotate the image, add a star to it, and start other Picasa options.

At any time in Picasa 3, you can reconfigure the file types that the Photo Viewer will display with the **Tools, Configure Photo Viewer** menu command. This opens the configuration box shown in **G37**. If you are not impressed, just select the **Don't use Picasa Photo Viewer** option, and it will go away.

* * *

You can do a lot more with Picasa and Web Albums, but we leave it to you to find out how. We have set out here to get you up to speed with the basics, and the rest really should be no problem to you. We hope you get as much enjoyment from Picasa as we do though!

12

YouTube

You**Tube**· These days people seem to have an incredible
desire to swap video clips with each other, and
that's where **YouTube** comes in. It is a video sharing Web
site, owned by Google, where anyone can view, upload, and
share video clips. According to Google, people are watching
hundreds of millions of videos a day on YouTube, so it's
really a huge repository of video clips. YouTube is free as it
is partially supported by advertising.

YouTube was first created in February 2005 but it caught
on very quickly and only 18 months later Google purchased
it for US$1.65 billion. By January 2008 nearly 79 million
YouTube users had made over 3 billion video viewings.

YouTube has become so popular so quickly mainly
because it is very easy to use. It accepts most common
video formats and converts them so that they can be viewed
over the Web without special software. So anybody can
upload video clips from their digital cameras or cell phones,
and friends can view them without worrying about the format.
You can also e-mail the link to friends easily, or add
YouTube generated code to your Web page or blog so a
video can be played from the page.

Finding Your Way Around

To start YouTube you can type **uk.youtube.com** into the
Address Bar of your browser and press the **Enter** key. Or
you can open it from the top of any Google page by clicking
the **more**, **YouTube** links. A page similar to ours in Fig. 12.1
should open.

Fig. 12.1 The Top Part of YouTube's Opening Screen

The Home Tab

Fig. 12.2 Search Suggestions

The YouTube screen opens on the **Home** tab, as shown above, with a **Search** box at the top. You enter text here to search YouTube for the type of video content you want to watch. This **Search** box has Google's search-suggest feature built in, so you get query suggestions as you type like the ones in Fig. 12.2. These apparently are based on the most popular search queries sent in to Google. They should save a few keystrokes, reduce spelling errors, and "improve the overall search experience".

A small 'cycling' selection of **Videos being watched right now** is displayed at the top of the Home page. Clicking any of these will open the video for you to watch. Below these is a selection of **Promoted** or sponsored videos. In other words, someone has paid to have them there. The BBC very often has advert and information videos in this section.

The rest of the Home page has listings of **Featured**, **Most Viewed**, **Most Discussed** and **Top Favorited** videos. **Featured** videos are selected by YouTube editors who review highly-rated and recent videos.

Masks
A short film we made to open the Shetland Film Festival! The film examines the destruction...
(more)

From: Maddrim
Views: 17,112
★★★★☆
04:34

More in Film & Animation

Fig. 12.3 The Layout of a Typical Featured Video Listing

Each video listed has a title and image (you can click either to watch the video), a short description and some statistics, as shown in Fig. 12.3.

The Videos Tab

The **Videos** tab is where you can more rapidly get a feel for YouTube. This has a links list of video **Categories** (Fig. 12.4), and two menu bars above the offered videos.

| All |
| Autos & Vehicles |
| Comedy |
| Education |
| Entertainment |
| Film & Animation |
| Gaming |
| Howto & Style |
| Music |
| News & Politics |
| People & Blogs |
| Pets & Animals |
| Science & Technology |
| Sports |
| Travel & Events |

G45 in Colour Gallery **2** shows how these can be used to effect. It shows the **Most Viewed** option selected on the top bar and the **All Time** option on the second bar. At the time of writing these were the eight most viewed videos in YouTube. Nearly 67 million times for one of them!

Fig. 12.4

The Channels Tab

In YouTube a **Channel** is a customised user's page, containing a user's profile information, videos, favorites and whatever else they want to share. YouTube is so popular now that its users are not only individuals publishing short clips, but large corporate bodies, the Queen, universities and public departments. They consider YouTube to be a modern way to get their messages across. The BBC Channel in Fig. 12.5 on the next page is an example of one of these.

Fig. 12.5 The BBC's Channel on YouTube

The Community Tab

YouTube largely consists of a community of people who enjoy engaging with each other by watching and uploading videos and commenting on them. On the **Community** tab you can browse groups, contests, help forums and blogs. Groups allow users to share videos and have discussions on a common theme and contests are where users submit videos to contests and other users can vote on them.

For a new user perhaps the most useful section is the **Community Help Forums**. This includes **Announcements**, where YouTube announces new features, and **How do I...?**, where you can find answers to questions about YouTube that you couldn't find in Help. You can **Post** questions and get replies and answers from expert users.

Your Own YouTube Account

Unregistered users can watch most videos on the site, but by registering, you can upload and share videos, save favorites, create a channel and playlists, and comment on videos. In other words, to get the most from YouTube you need to Sign Up.

This is easy to do. Clicking the **Sign Up** link at the top of a page (shown in colour in **G46**) opens the following box.

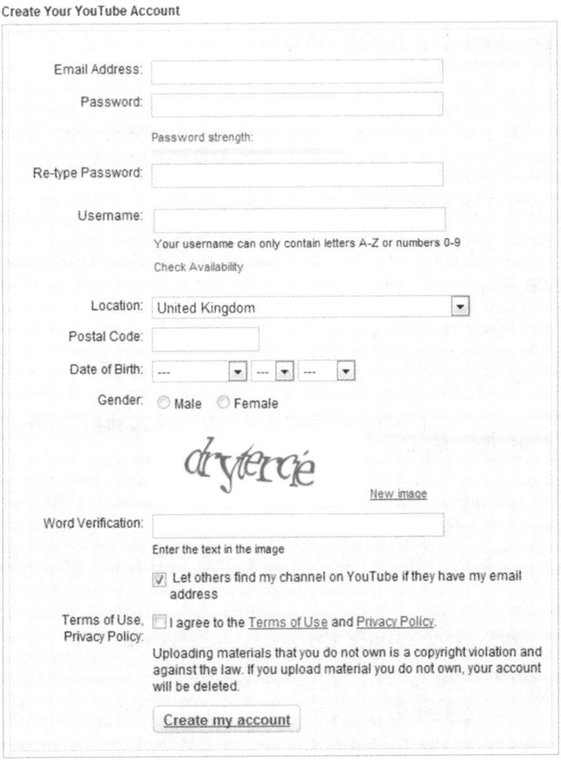

Fig. 12.6 Creating an Account in YouTube

Just fill in the text boxes, tick the box to agree to the copyright and Privacy Policy, and click on the **Create my account** button.

Once you have done this you can sign in to YouTube at any time from the Sign In link at the top of most pages. This opens the standard entry box shown in Fig. 12.7 for you to enter your Username and Password.

Fig. 12.7 The Sign In Box

Some Technical Stuff

Videos on YouTube are streamed through an Adobe Flash player. To get the best results, we suggest you install the latest version of Adobe Flash from the Adobe Web site at:

www.adobe.com/products/flashplayer

YouTube say the minimum requirements to watch videos on their site are:

Flash Player 7.0+ plug-in.
Windows 2000 or higher with latest updates installed.
Mac OS X 10.3 or higher.
Firefox 1.1+, Internet Explorer 5.0+ or Safari 1.0+.
Broadband connection with 500+ Kbps.

If this is you, we strongly recommend you upgrade everything as soon as possible! Like everything else these days, YouTube works best on a state of the art computer.

Standard and High Quality Videos

A standard quality YouTube video has a picture 320 pixels wide by 240 pixels high and uses the Sorenson Spark H.263 video codec. The bit rate of the video signal is around 314 kbit/s with a frame rate dependent on the uploaded video. In March 2008, YouTube launched a **High Quality** format feature which allows some videos to be viewed at 480x360 pixels. They decide if videos are capable of this improved quality based on the standard of the original upload.

You can set up YouTube to switch automatically to this better quality on your YouTube Account page, as shown in Fig. 12.8 below. To open your Account page select **more** from the **Account** drop-down menu, shown open below. In the **Account** section, click on **Video Playback Quality**, select **I have a fast connection. Always show me higher quality when available** and click the **Save Settings** button. You should of course only do this if you have a fast Internet connection, or videos won't play properly!

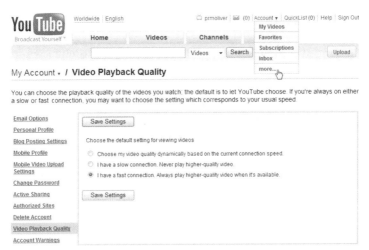

Fig. 12.8 Setting Video Playback Quality in My Account

This means that you have to be signed in to YouTube for the setting to be effective. But provided the user you're watching uploaded a high quality video, you should be able to force it to display in high quality even when you are not signed in.

The trick is to append **&fmt=18** to the end of the URL in your browser's Address Bar, as shown for a typical example below. This increases the resolution from the normal 320x240 pixels to 480x360.

http://uk.youtube.com/watch?v=gYrZPaSNPw8**&fmt=18**

Watching Videos

As we have seen, to watch a video you just click its thumbnail image or title link. **G46** shows a typical YouTube video of one of our favourite soccer players after scoring a goal. Below the picture area is a toolbar which gives you some control.

Fig. 12.9 Video Playing Toolbar

Clicking the **Play** button ▶ starts the video and changes to the **Pause** button ‖. With the **Slider**, you can move quickly through a video and see where you are with the numbers to the right. In our example above the slider is at the end of a 33 second video. To vary the sound level, you click the **Volume** button 🔊 and use the slider that opens. You can view videos in a window or in full screen mode with the ▬ button. The **Annotations** button 🔺 lets you turn on or off the annoying annotations, or messages, in some videos.

A selection of **Related** (or similar) videos appears on the right of a playing video, with others sent by the same user. If you click the Subscribe button you will be able to keep track of your favourite users new videos.

Below a playing video are four buttons shown in Fig. 12.10. The **Share** option gives you several ways of sharing the video with your peers. You can add the current video as a **Favorite**, add it to a **Playlist**, or **Flag** it for inappropriate content.

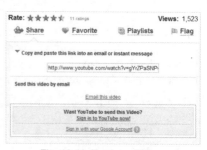

Fig. 12.10 Sharing a Video

To watch your **Favorites** later, just go to the **Account** link at the top of the page and choose **Favorites**.

Colour Gallery 2

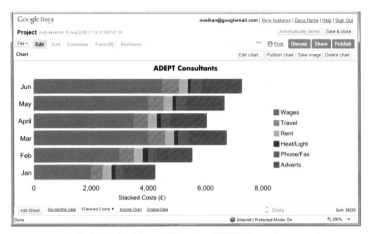

G32 A Stacked Costs Chart for ADEPT Consultants

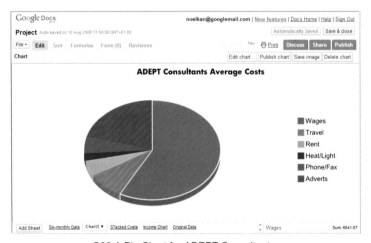

G33 A Pie Chart for ADEPT Consultants

G34 Presentation Templates

G35 Modified Presentation Template

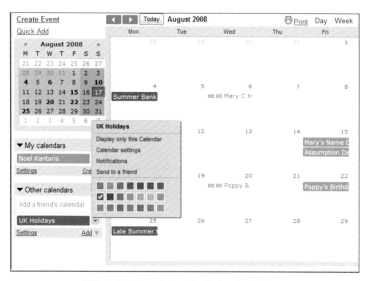

G36 Selecting a Colour for Calendar Entries

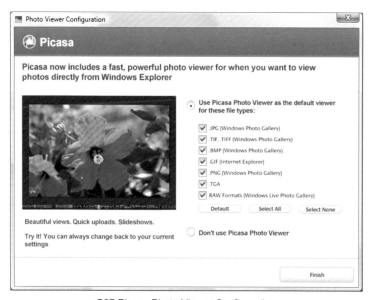

G37 Picasa Photo Viewer Configuration

G38 Working with Photos in Picasa

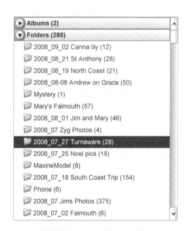

G39 Picasa Folder List in
Flat Folder Structure View

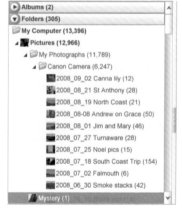

G40 Picasa Folder List in
Tree View

G41 Editing a Zoomed-in Photo in Picasa

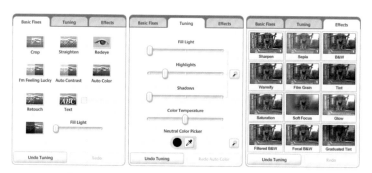

G42 The Photo Editing Features Available in Picasa

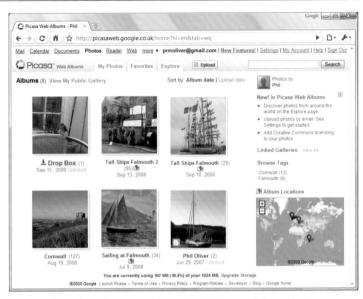

G43 One of our Spaces on Picasa Web Albums – Viewed in Chrome

G44 The Picasa Photo Viewer Working in a Window

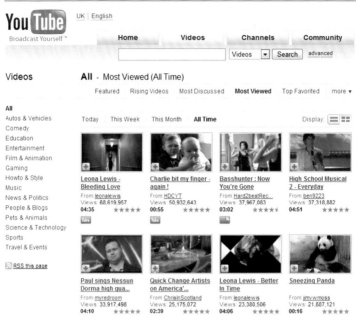

G45 The Most Viewed Videos of All Time on YouTube

G46 Playing a High Quality Video on YouTube

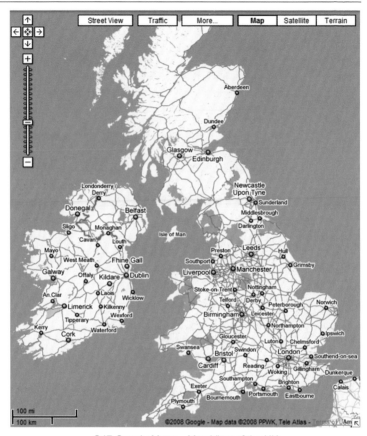

G47 Google Maps – Map View of the UK

G48 Google Maps – Map View of Southampton at Maximum Zoom

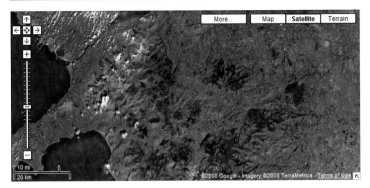

G49 Google Maps – North Wales in Satellite View

G50 Google Maps – North Wales in Satellite View with Labels

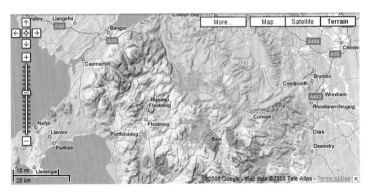

G51 Google Maps – North Wales in Terrain View

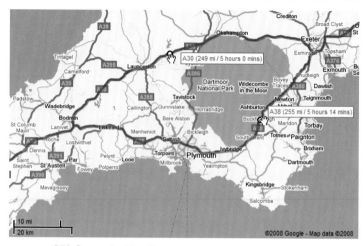

G52 Comparing Two Routes Interactively in Google Maps

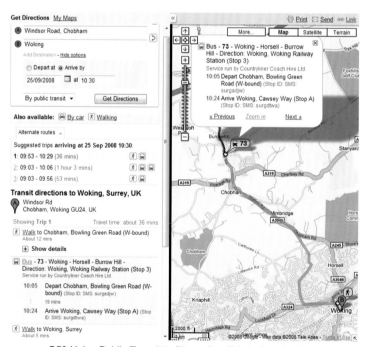

G53 Using Public Transit to Plan a Bus Trip in Google Maps

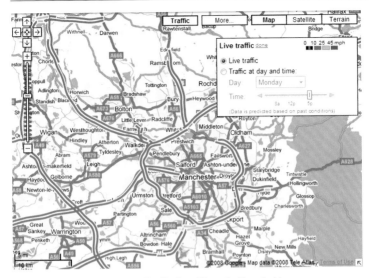

G54 Checking Traffic Conditions in Google Maps

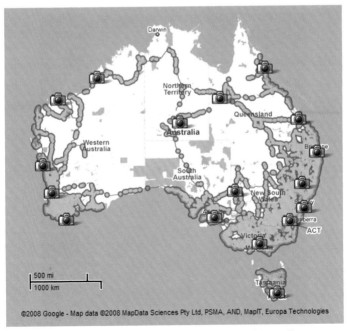

G55 Google Maps - Street View Coverage of Australia

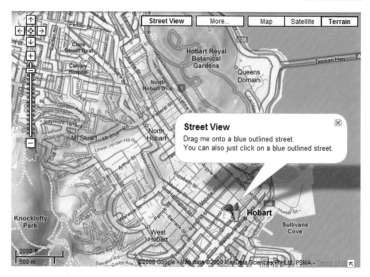

G56 Google Maps - Zoomed in to show Street View of Hobart, Australia

G57 Part of the Opening View in Google Earth

G58 Zooming in on a London Street in Google Earth

G59 The Places Panel

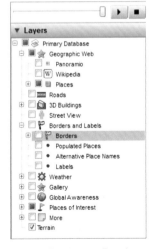

G60 The Layers Panel

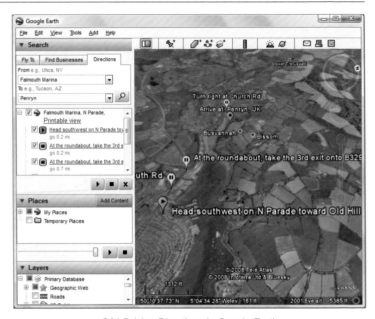

G61 Driving Directions in Google Earth

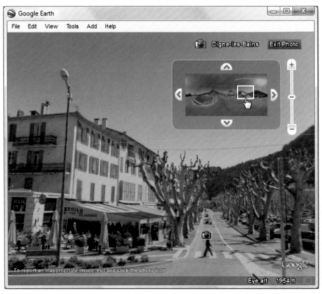

G62 Google Earth - Street View Coverage in France

G63 Google Moon Home Page in the Google Chrome Browser

G64 Installing the Google Chrome Browser

G65 Chrome's New Tab Page

G66 The Google Chrome Opening Web Page

Save to QuickList

 A QuickList is a way to grab videos that look interesting as you browse the YouTube site. This puts them into a temporary playlist to watch later. You add a video to your QuickList by clicking the grey ✚ icon on the video's thumbnail image. The ✚ icon then turns to the **Added** link.

To view your QuickList, just click on an **Added** link, or click on the **QuickList** link at the top of the page. From the QuickList page, you can watch all the videos in the list, delete them, or save the list as a permanent Playlist.

Viewing History

If you want to re-watch a video you watched earlier in the same session, click the **QuickList** link at the top of the screen and select **History** from the menu on the left. The list of videos that displays in your Viewing History will disappear when you close your Web browser.

Downloading Videos

YouTube itself does not currently have a way of letting you download videos from its site. This is easy to do, though, you just have to use realPlayer. Go to **www.realplayer.com** and download the free version of realPlayer. Once it is installed, whenever you play a video on YouTube you should see the above **Download This Video** icon. Click it, and a box will pop up that shows the progress of the download. You can then play the video at any time using realPlayer.

Your Own Videos

It is remarkably easy to put your own videos on YouTube, but they are limited to just over ten minutes in length, and a file size of 1GB. Ideally your source video needs to be high resolution, such as MOV or AVI file, NTSC 720x480 or VGA 640x480. YouTube converts videos into the Flash Video format after uploading, so it is important to keep an aspect ratio of 4:3, otherwise the quality of the video will be degraded. YouTube recommends the following for a video:

MPEG4 (DivX, Xvid) format.
640x480 resolution.
64k Mono or 128k Stereo MP3 audio.
30 frames per second.
Up to 1GB file size and 10 min. duration.

Uploading Your Video

Once you've finished making and editing your video, just click the **Upload** button [Upload] in the upper-right-hand corner of any YouTube page.

Enter as much information about your video as possible, including a **Title**, **Description**, **Tags**, and **Category**. The more information you include, the easier it will be for users to find it! Choose whether you want your video set to **Public** or **Private**. If you make it private the only people that will be able to view it are those you have given permission.

Clicking the **Upload a Video** button opens a new window in which you click the **Browse** button to select the video file you want to upload. Finally click the **Upload Video** button.

Clicking the **Use Quick Capture** button lets you record and upload a video instantly with your Webcam.

Whichever method you use and depending on its size, it can take from a couple minutes to hours for a video to upload to YouTube and be processed. Have fun.

Fig. 12.11 Using a Webcam

13

Google Maps

Anyone who has ever loved maps should certainly not skip our next two chapters which cover Google's two map-based tools. **Google Maps** gives a flat 2D view of the world both in map and satellite image format, while **Google Earth** gives a 3D view of the planet by joining satellite, aerial and street level photography and mapping.

You can use Google Maps to search for locations and addresses, to find local businesses, to get driving or walking directions, or just to enjoy looking at its maps and satellite views. Most of Google Maps functions are available in the UK and Europe and its satellite imagery covers the entire World, but at varying levels of resolution (or quality). The map data for the UK is Based on Ordnance Survey electronic data and is provided by Tele Atlas.

The Google Maps Environment

Google Maps is another example of 'cloud computing' as you do your map viewing in a Web browser and everything is downloaded from the Internet. The maps load very quickly, but a fast broadband connection certainly helps.

Once your browser is open you can open Google Maps in one of several ways. You can type **maps.google.co.uk** into the Address bar of your browser and press the **Enter** key, you can click the **Maps** link at the top of any Google UK page, or you can force Maps to open with the location you want by typing the location, or post code, followed by '**map**' into a Google Web Search box, as described on page 20. With the first methods the opening window should look like that in Fig. 13.1 on the next page.

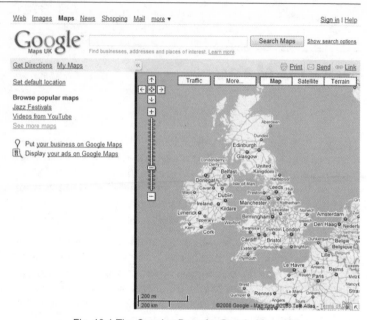

Fig. 13.1 The Opening Page for Google Maps UK

If you get an opening map of the USA it means you started from a US Google page, not a UK one.

Map Views

Depending on your location, there are different map views available in Google Maps. These are controlled by the buttons across the top of the map area, as shown above. You click these buttons to change between the views:

Map – This shows a traditional style of map with a depiction of roads, borders, rivers, parks and lakes, etc. **G47** and **G48** in Colour Gallery 2 show clear examples of this map view at different zoom levels.

Satellite – This shows satellite and aerial imagery of the same area. To show road and street names and other information, click **Satellite**, **Show Labels**. The satellite images are not current and their quality depends on the locality. See **G49** and **G50** for colour examples.

Terrain – This shows physical features on the map, such as rivers, mountains and parkland. Elevation is shown as shaded relief with contours when you are zoomed in. It also includes road numbers, street names and other information, as we show in **G51**.

More – This superimposes location-specific photos and Wikipedia articles on an existing map view. Sometimes, unless you zoom right in these can obliterate the map.

Traffic – Provides visual traffic data for motorways and major trunk roads in England. This feature was added as we were writing the chapter!

Street View – In some locations, you can view and navigate within wrap around street-level imagery.

The last two buttons only appear if the feature is available for anywhere on the open map area.

Searching for a Location

If you want to find details of a particular location you just search for it. This is a Google program after all! You can search for an address, city, town, airport, county, country or continent by typing details in the search box and clicking **Search Maps**, as shown below.

Fig. 13.2 Entering a Search Address

The result of this search is shown in Fig. 13.3 on the next page. Google jumped to a map of the Cornish town, placed a Marker and Info Window on it and showed the search result in text in the left pane of the page also with a marker.

For specific addresses, entering them in the form of **Address, town, post code** usually gives the best results. You can also search for geographic features such as parks, mountains, lakes, etc., in the same way.

Fig. 13.3 The Result of a Search for a Town

As shown in Fig. 13.3, the left pane can display photos, videos, and community maps based on the current map location. Clicking the **Explore this area** link overlays tiny geocoded thumbnail images onto the map and displays arrays of photos, videos, and community maps that are found within the currently visible map boundary. A nice touch is that as you pan and zoom your map (see next page) everything updates dynamically, adding, removing, and reordering the videos, pictures, and maps available based on the new map area. Very slick.

To get more map viewing area, you can collapse the left panel by clicking on the double arrow « icon that appears above the top left corner of the map. Clicking it again will reopen the pane.

To get even more map room, maximise the window and go to your browser's **Full Screen** mode. With Internet Explorer and Firefox browsers you do this with the **F11** key. Others may be different.

Searching for a Business

No matter where you are in the country, as long as you have Google Maps you can always find the nearest, or most convenient, businesses or services. As you might expect, you use the Search Box for this. Just enter the type of business or service, followed by the words **in** or **near**, and the town, city or other location.

In Fig. 13.4, when our dog needed help, we typed **vets in redruth** and pressed the **Search Maps** button.

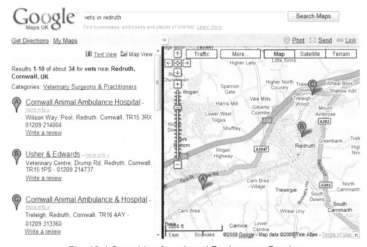

Fig. 13.4 Searching for a Local Business or Service

Google worked out that we meant to search for 'Vetinary Surgeons & Practioners' and showed the results of the search in the left panel and a map of the area in the right panel with markers linked to the results.

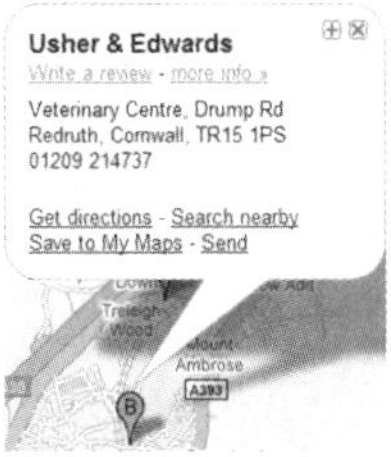

If you click a marker, either alongside an entry in the left panel or on the map, an info window opens with details of that business and a set of useful action links, as shown here in Fig. 13.5.

Fig. 13.5

Navigating the Map Area

With Google Maps you can change what shows in the map viewing area in two dimensions. You can pan the map (move it across the screen at the same scale), and you can zoom it in (to see a smaller area in more detail) or out (to see a larger area with less detail).

Using the Mouse

We find it much easier and quicker to do all these operations with the mouse. To pan the map, just hold the left mouse button down and drag the map around the screen. To zoom, just roll the mouse wheel away from you to zoom in, and towards you to zoom out. The zoom will centre on the pointer location on the map. With these actions you can almost instantly zoom out to view the whole Earth, move the pointer to a new location and zoom in again to the scale you need. You can also centre and zoom in on a location, by double-clicking it on the map.

Using the Navigation Controls

The navigation controls shown here are placed in the top left corner of Google maps. These also work well and rely on you clicking, or dragging, them with your mouse.

To pan the map, you click the arrow buttons in the top grouping.

Click ⬆ to move the map North, ⬇ to move the map South, ➡ to move it East, or ⬅ to move it West. Clicking the ✳ icon in the centre will return you to your original view.

The bottom grouping has zoom controls.

Click ➕ to zoom in on the centre of the map, and ➖ to zoom out. Dragging the zoom slider ▭ up or down will zoom in or out incrementally.

Using the Keyboard

If you prefer using the keyboard, you can zoom in and out with the **+** and **–** keys. You can pan left ⇐, right ⇒, up ⇧, and down ⇩ with the arrow keys. These only move the map a little, so for larger pans you can use the **Page Up**, **Page Down**, **Home**, and **End** keys to move North, South, East and West. Holding down any of these keys will keep the map scrolling across your screen.

Using the Overview Map

Fig. 13.6 The Overview Map

The overview map appears in the bottom right corner of the map. It shows the location of the current map view as a purple box in a larger geographical area. You can change the view in the main map by dragging the purple box in the overview map. To hide the overview map click the ⌐⌐ icon, to display it again click on ⌐⌐.

Getting Directions

There are several ways in Google Maps to get directions from one location to another.

Type a **from-to** statement into the search field, such as **from redruth to woking**, and click **Search Maps**.

Click **Get Directions**, enter a starting and ending location and click the **Get Directions** button.

Get directions from an info window (See Fig. 13.3).

Right-click on the map to get directions to that location.

The first method actually completes the operation as if you had used the second method, as shown in Fig. 13.7 on the next page.

Fig. 13.7 Getting Driving Directions

The program defaults to giving driving directions and the recommended route appears on the map as a blue line with markers at either end as shown above. Google Maps breaks down its detailed directions into numbered sections in the left panel, and gives a total distance and estimated driving time above them. You can click on any section number in the left

Fig. 13.8 Info Window

panel to display an info window on the map with instructions for that section.

In the **Get Directions** box you can get new directions that **Avoid highways** (motorways in the UK) or **Avoid tolls**. To reverse the directions for the return trip, click the ⬧ button. To change the starting or ending locations just retype them. To add a new location to the route, click the **Add destination** link to open another entry box, type in the location, and drag the box into the list wherever you want it. To delete a location click the grey × on its right.

To change the distance units for directions, click **km** (kilometres) or **miles**. After making any changes in the box make sure you click the **Get Directions** button.

To get more map area, don't forget you can collapse the left panel by clicking on the double arrow « icon that appears above the top left corner of the map. Clicking it again will re-open the pane.

When you study the proposed route on the map you may find you want to alter it. That's no problem with Google Maps. You can just click and drag any point on the purple directions line to any location of the map. Before you let go of the pointer a message flag shows the new distance and time for the trip taking that route. If you accept the new routing Google Maps immediately re-creates the directions on both the map and left panel. The point you added appears as a white dot on the route. As an example of this we compared the section between Bodmin and Exeter for our route from Cornwall to the London area. As shown in colour in **G52**, the two routes were the A30 North of Dartmoor and the A38 South of the Moor. As you can see the A30 is just the best! This is very clever indeed.

Walking Directions

Google Maps will now give walking directions if you select **Walking** from the drop-down menu in the **Get Directions** box, after entering the start and end locations as before. If you request walking directions, Google Maps tries to find you a route that is direct, flat, and uses pedestrian pathways when Google know about them.

Fig. 13.9 on the next page shows an example walking route. We have tried this feature for several local walks that we know about. The routes suggested usually follow minor roads and tracks, rather than footpaths as we know them. It didn't recognise the Camel Trail, Cornwall's most visited attraction. Still it's better than nothing and it is still in beta. Google Maps advises you to "use caution and always obey all signs or notices regarding your route".

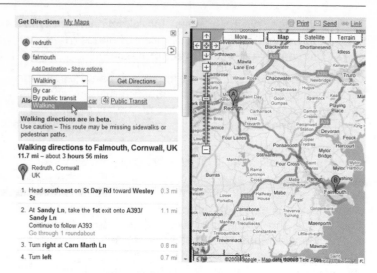

Fig. 13.9 Getting Walking Directions

Public Transport

Depending on where you are, the **Public Transit** feature of Google Maps may allow you to map and plan your trip using public bus and coach transport. At the time of writing, Google Transit could plan trips in the UK on Traveline Southeast, and nationally on long-distance coach services. To look for updates on this, you could try **www.google.com/transit**.

If transit information is available when you search for directions between start and end locations in Google Maps, the **By public transit** option will appear in the **Get Directions** box, as we show in colour in **G53**.

To find the times of the next three buses available on the route, select the **By public transit** option and just click the **Get Directions** button. To plan your trip in the future, click the **Show options** link and set your date and time choices in the sub-pane that opens, as we did in **G53**.

One thing to watch though, is that long-distance coach services are sometimes offered for a short trip. This can create some confusing and long routes!

Printing Google Maps

You can print **Map View** maps and direction information in Google Maps, but you can't print terrain maps or satellite imagery. With the map area you want to print on the screen you click the **Print** link at the top right of the window. A very clever interactive print preview page opens for you to customise what you print. If **Get Directions** is active in the left panel it will have the same format as Fig. 13.10 below. If **My Maps** is active you will just be offered the current map.

Fig. 13.10 Interactive Print Preview of Driving Directions

You can add notes in the text box at the top, and drag or zoom the map to get the view you want to print. If you are printing directions, as in Fig. 13.10, you can click **Maps** in the bar at the top to display thumbnails with the directions. You can drag the map in each of these thumbnails, or click ⊞ to zoom in, ⊟ to zoom out, or ⊠ to close it. Very clever.

To show the original map view with a set of directions, check the **Include large map** option in the top bar. When you have finished playing with these features, click the **Print** button to open the Print box for you to send everything to your printer.

If you are very lucky and the **Street View** option appears in the top bar of the Print Preview window, you can select this to put interactive photos in your printed directions.

Fig. 13.11 Street View Photos Included in a Print Preview

You can pan each of these photos through 360° by dragging the mouse pointer, or holding down the left or right arrow keys on the keyboard.

Sharing Maps

If you click **Send** at the top of the Google Maps main window you can e-mail the current map or directions to a friend or colleague. The **Link** option next to it opens a box with two sets of code. You can copy each of these and **Paste link..** in the body of an e-mail message, or **Paste HTML** to embed the code for the current map in a Web page.

Traffic View

Google Maps has just added an exciting new traffic feature, that provides traffic data for the motorways and major A roads in England, but not yet Scotland and Wales.

Fig. 13.12 The Traffic View Info Window

Whatever map view you are in, if you click the **Traffic** button the parts of motorways and trunk roads that are subject to traffic hold ups will be overlayed with colour. If you are zoomed too far out, as in our case above, traffic light icons appear. If you click on one of these, an info window opens with its location and a **Zoom In** link. Clicking this, zooms you in to show current traffic speeds directly on the map, as in our colour example in **G54**, for the Manchester area.

If your route shows red, its stop-and-go for you, yellow, shows slower than normal traffic, and green means it is probably clear. You can also select **Traffic at day and time** in the open box, to get predictions of likely conditions. When you are finished, click the **Traffic** button again to turn it off.

Street View

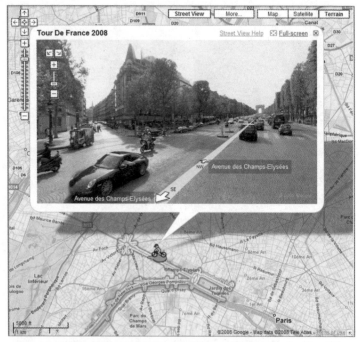

Street View gives navigable 360° street-level imagery in Google Maps, and also in Google Earth. To obtain the imagery, Google sends specially **Peg Man** adapted camera cars along the streets and roads to be covered, and these take full panoramic photos every few yards along the route. In Google Maps you can see images for each spot and take virtual walks or drives along that street. This lets you see what an area actually looks like, as if you were there in person, as shown below.

Fig. 13.13 Street View of the Champs-Elysées, Paris, showing Peg Man

Currently, Street View is available for the major US, Australian, French and Japanese cities. Google added Street View imagery for the 2008 Tour de France routes, which is what we have used in Fig. 13.13 above.

As this is being written, Google cars are photographing all over Europe, including the UK, and they plan to extend Street View coverage in the near future. Privacy problems permitting!

Like the **Traffic** button, the **Street View** button only shows if the feature is available anywhere in the open map area. When you click it, roads covered by Street View appear with

Fig. 13.14 The Camera Icon

a blue border. Clicking the button again will close the feature. When you are zoomed out a camera icon also appears at available locations, as shown in **G55**. If you click on one of these, an info window opens with its location and a **Zoom In** link, as in Fig. 13.14.

Clicking this link will zoom the map so that individual streets are visible, as in **G56**, and place the 'Peg Man' icon on it. We have also seen Peg Man dressed as a cyclist and a clown, but he is bound to come up with other disguises over time.

Clicking Peg Man, or clicking any street with a blue border, or dragging him to one, will open Street View for that location in a window overlay, as shown in Fig. 13.13. The green arrow under Peg Man shows the direction Street View

Fig. 13.15 Street View Controls

is looking.

You can rotate the view by dragging it right or left with your mouse, with the right and left arrow keys, or by clicking the pivot arrows buttons. To zoom in or out, drag the slider, click the **+** or **−** buttons, or double-click a point on the image to zoom in on it.

To move along a street, click one of the arrows on the white or yellow direction line overlaid on the street as shown in Fig. 13.15 and 13.16. The ⇑ and ⇓ arrow keys can also be used for this.

Fig. 13.16 Street View of One of Our Holiday Locations in Australia

As shown here, street names display within the info window, and in most locations the approximate street address is shown above it. Below the info window, Street View's Peg Man moves around the underlying map. For larger moves you can drag and drop him on a blue bordered road.

Once you have found the area you want to explore with **Street View**, we suggest you click **Full-screen** to view a larger Street View area. We have a large monitor and prefer to explore in our browser's **Full Screen** mode, by clicking the **F11** key. To shrink an expanded info window, click the ⊟ button, and to close it click the ⊠ button.

As you may have gathered, we use this feature a lot, especially when we are planning a vacation. If you ever find something inappropriate on Street View you should report it to Google. To do this, click the **Street View Help** link at the top of the 'offending' image window and the **Report inappropriate image** link at the bottom of the opened box.

Default Location

The default view that Google Maps displays is determined by your location. That for the UK is shown in Fig. 13.1. If you

Fig. 13.17 A Default Location

prefer to use a different starting location, click the **Set default location** link in the left panel, enter an address in the search box and click **Save**. You can change it in the future by clicking **Change default location.**

Your preference is actually stored on your computer in a cookie, so if you delete 'your cookies' you will go back to square one! The default location can also get lost whenever you sign in to your Google account.

Creating a Map

If you have a Google account and are signed in you can create customised maps using Google Maps. You can add placemarks 📍, lines 〰, shapes 🔲, and text, and embed photos and videos in your map.

To create a map, click **My Maps** in the left panel, click the **Create new map** link and add a title and description for your map. Set the map area and view you want for your map in the mapping area and use the icons in the top left corner of the map to customise it. We will leave the rest for you to experiment with, but have given a very simple example of the process in Fig. 13.18 on the next page. The video below may be a good place to start.

www.google.com/help/maps/tour/#create_a_map

You can make your maps **Public** so they will be included in everyone else's Google Maps and Google Earth search results, or **Unlisted** so that only you or anyone you want can view them.

Fig. 13.18 The Makings of a Customised Google Map

As long as you are signed in you can return to your map at any time by clicking the **My Maps** link and selecting it.

Mobile Maps

If you have a suitable Java-enabled mobile phone, you can visit **www.google.com/gmm** to download **Google Maps for mobile**.

Hot off the press while this was still being written is the launch of the new G1 mobile phone working on Android, Google's new operating system for mobiles. Google Maps on this is outstanding. Not only does it load maps quickly and beautifully, but has a 'compass mode' that shows Street View facing the direction you are travelling at the moment. Very exciting, but whether we will ever be able to afford to run one is a different matter!

14

Google Earth

 Google Earth gives an interactive globe on your computer. It streams Earth information, such as images, elevations, business data, etc., to computers over the Internet. Using it, you can zoom and glide over satellite photos of the world, find driving directions or nearby restaurants, measure the distance between two locations, do serious research, or go on virtual vacations. As a user you can explore the Earth and zoom down to cities, points of interest, buildings, bridges, roads and natural features, and it's fun.

The Technology

When you open Google Earth on your computer, you appear to zoom in from outer space. In fact you seamlessly go through a succession of closer and closer photos, from NASA shuttle shots, to satellite shots, to high resolution photos taken from an aircraft.

Google uses various suppliers of images. At the bottom of the screen are names like AeroWest, Cnes/Spot Image, DigitalGlobe, GeoContent, GeoEye, NASA and Terra Metrics. But they put it all together with their own software to give the seamless zooming-in effect.

It is reported that Google has recently signed a deal with GeoEye to provide imagery from the GeoEye-1 satellite which was launched in September 2008 with the Google logo on the side of the rocket. This satellite orbits 423 miles above the Earth and provides the highest ground resolution colour imagery commercially available at the moment.

Many other companies supply Google with images taken from aircraft and they have their own software to fit all these images together, like a gigantic panoramic image.

Versions of Google Earth

There are three main versions of Google Earth. The free version, for Windows (Vista, XP, 2000), Mac (OS X 10.4), and Linux, intended for personal, non-commercial use. Google Earth Plus with GPS support, data importing and higher resolution printing, and Google Earth Pro for professional and commercial use. Most users will only require the free version and we only cover its features here.

System Requirements

To run Google Earth in Windows you will need at least:

A PC with Windows 2000, Windows XP, or Windows Vista, with a Pentium 3 500Mhz processor, 256MB of RAM, 400MB of free hard disc space, a network speed of 128 Kbits/sec, a 3D-capable graphics card with 16MB of VRAM, 1024x768 screen using16-bit High Colour and DirectX 9 (to run in Direct X mode).

But a more realistic configuration as recommended by Google would be:

A PC with Windows XP, or Windows Vista, with a Pentium 4 2.4GHz+ or AMD 2400xp+ processor, 512MB of RAM, 2GB of free hard disc space, a network speed of 768 Kbits/sec, a 3D-capable graphics card with 32MB of VRAM, 1280x1024 screen using 32-bit True Colour.

Downloading Google Earth

Although the data for Google Earth is streamed over the Internet, the program itself has to be downloaded from Google. To get it, go to **http://earth.google.com** which opens the screen shown in Fig. 14.1 below. When you have looked around the page, press the **Download..** button to start the process.

Fig. 14.1 Starting the Google Earth Download Procedure

Read the License Agreement on the next page and click **Agree and Download**. When you are asked if you want to Run or **Save** the file select **Run** and follow any instructions.

Google Earth   The final box of the process is shown in Fig. 14.2. This lets you send data to Google if you don't object, and starts Google Earth for the first time. To start the program in the future, just double-click on your new Desktop icon shown above.

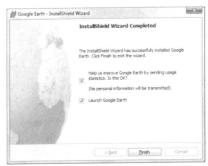

Fig. 14.2 A Successful Installation

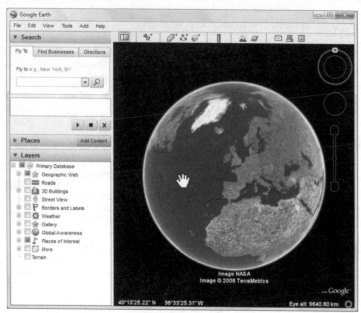

Fig. 14.3 The Google Earth Starting Window

The Google Earth Interface

Google Earth opens with a view of the Earth from space, as shown above and in **G57**. This appears in the right section of the program's window known as the **3D viewer** which is always open. On the left side of the window is a sidebar with three panels. The **Search** panel is used to find places and directions and manage search results. The **Places** panel is used to locate, save and organise placemarks, and the **Layers** panel lets you 'switch on and off' available layers which display specific features in the 3D viewer.

To get more room for the 3D viewer, you can close the sidebar by clicking the **Hide Sidebar** button on the toolbar below the Google Earth menu bar. To show the sidebar when it is closed just click the button again.

Navigating the Globe

Dragging the left mouse button 🖑 on the globe will gently rotate it in the direction you drag. On a flat map this is the panning action. Double-clicking the mouse buttons, rotating the middle scroll wheel, or dragging the right mouse button, will zoom you in or out. If you drag the mouse with the middle scroll wheel depressed you can tilt the globe. We find these are the easiest ways to 'get around' the Earth, and suggest you practise them on the whole globe, as it is easier to see the results.

Navigation Controls

If you move the pointer over the upper right-hand corner of the 3D viewer, the Navigation Controls change from an unobtrusive outline, as shown in Fig. 14.3, to the full version, shown here. These offer the same type of navigation action as the mouse but you can also swoop and rotate your view.

The **Look** joystick at the top lets you look around from a single vantage point. Click an arrow to look in that direction or press down on the arrow to change your view. Dragging the outer ring rotates the view. Clicking the **North-up** button resets it with North at the top.

The **Move** joystick, in the middle, moves your position from one place to another. Click an arrow to look in that direction or press down on the mouse button to change your view. After clicking an arrow, move the mouse around on the joystick to change the direction of motion.

Dragging the **Zoom** slider ▭ up or down will zoom in or out incrementally, or click ⊞ to zoom in on the centre of the 3D viewer, and ⊟ to zoom out. As you move closer to the ground, Google Earth tilts to change your viewing angle to be parallel to the Earth's surface. You have to play with all these to get used to their actions.

Navigating on the Ground

With version 4.3 of Google Earth you can navigate at ground level. We will step through an example to explain this and generally get you started.

Fig. 14.4 Search Panel

First type **London** in the **Fly To** box of Google Earth's **Search** panel and click the **Begin Search** button 🔍. This will place a somewhat fuzzy image of London, taken from 24.75 miles up, into the 3D viewer. Now for the fun bit. Place the pointer on the **+** button of the Zoom slider and keep pressing it. This will smoothly zoom you in to St Margaret St, London, and as it gets nearer the ground will tilt the view, as shown in colour in **G58**. When it stops you are just above ground level and can navigate around with the keyboard arrow keys. (Use **Alt+** arrow keys to move more slowly).

This is not quite up to Street View, but it can still be fun, and you should now be happy with the Zoom slider buttons!

Some Sightseeing

Fig. 14.5 The Places Panel

While you are still looking around, find the **Sightseeing** folder in the **Places** panel shown open in Fig. 14.5 and in colour in **G59**. You may need to scroll down to view this folder. If necessary, open it by clicking the **+** button next to it. Google provides you with some well known places to visit. In fact, we have deleted some here to give us more room.

Double-clicking an entry will zoom Google Earth to that location. Try it.

If you select the folder itself and press the **Play** button ▶ below, it will work its way through the list, zooming in to each location.

My Places

As we saw in Fig. 14.5 the **Places** panel contains two main folders, My Places and Temporary Places. You can use the My Places folder to save and organise places that you visit, address searches and natural features.

Setting Placemarks

The first location most people would want to 'placemark' in Google Earth is their home. This is very easy. First find the position you want in the 3D viewer, either by searching, or just zooming in the hard way. Choose the best viewing level for the location and click the **Placemark** button ℅⁺ on the toolbar at the top of the window.

Fig. 14.6 Setting a Placemark

The **New Placemark** box opens and a New Placemark icon is placed in the 3D viewer inside a flashing yellow square. Drag the placemark to the location you want, as shown in Fig. 14.6, and fill in the open box. You should give the placemark a name, but the rest is up to you. You can also add a description and set the style, colour and opacity of the marker. Clicking the **OK** button sets your placemark in the 3D viewer and as a new entry in the **My Places** folder.

In the future when you want to go to this location, just double-click its entry in the **My Places** folder. You can always change a placemark by right-clicking it, selecting **Properties** and using the **Edit Placemark** box.

Saving Search Results

When you carry out a **Find Businesses** search, a listing results panel opens below the Search button with a folder containing the top 10 results in it. You can collapse this folder by clicking the – icon next to it. In the same Google Earth session, you can revisit your search by double-clicking an item in the search list, or you can clear the results by clicking the **Clear** button x .

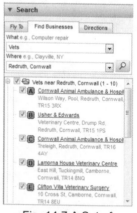

Fig. 14.7 A Set of Search Results

When you close Google Earth, your searches are cleared, but you can easily save search results for future use.

Simply drag a search result item from the search results panel and drop it in any folder in the **Places** panel. To save the contents of the entire search result to the **Places** panel drag the whole folder.

Once a search result is saved, you can change its title, location and description.

Getting Directions

Fig. 14.8 Driving Directions

To get directions in Google Earth is very similar to the procedure in Google Maps. The main way is to enter start and ending locations in the **Directions** tab and click the **Search** button ⌕. Route details and directions appear in the search listing window, as shown here in Fig. 14.8. The route is shown as a purple line in the 3D viewer, as shown in **G61**.

The easiest way to print your directions is to click the **Printable view** link in the **Search** panel. This opens your route in Google Maps for you to print, as described on Page 189.

Touring Your Route

Once you have a route displayed in the 3D viewer, you can use the **Tour** feature to 'overfly' the route in the 3D viewer. To do this, select the **Route** item at the end of the directions listing, and click the **Play Tour** button ▶. The 3D viewer will start the tour from the departure point, oriented in the correct direction as if you were flying over the route. The tour follows the route, stops at the end and zooms out to show the entire route in the 3D viewer.

Be warned though, Google Earth assumes you want to drive on the right side of the road, not a good idea in real life!

Saving Directions

When you close Google Earth, your directions are cleared, but you can easily save them for future use in the same way as described earlier for a set of search results.

Layers

Google Earth can provide a lot of information about a location, and viewed all at once, it would be very confusing. To get over this, it stores its information in layers, which you can turn on or off. Layers include data for such things as roads, borders, labels, restaurant guides, street names, and 3D buildings for select cities.

Layers are created by Google or its partners and are stored in the **Layers** panel area on the lower left-hand side of Google Earth, shown in **G60**. You turn on a layer by clicking the check-box next to its name and turn it off by removing the tick in the check box.

You should explore the content of the **Layers** panel by opening up all the folders and trying each option in turn. The **Gallery** folder contains some amazing very high resolution photography, and much more. In the **Places of Interest** (POI) folder you can get Google Earth to show you specific types of places, such as schools, banks, petrol stations, etc., the list is very long and more are being added all the time.

One thing to remember is that the amount of detail displayed in Google Earth at one time is dependent on your viewing height. As you zoom in on an area the detail will get more specific, so you always have to 'play around' a little.

Terrain and 3D Buildings

Two layers are useful for creating a more three dimensional globe. **Terrain** shows the 3D elevation of your current view. This is limited to natural geographic features, like mountains and canyons, and does not apply to buildings. Make sure it is selected before exploring any mountainous regions.

The **3D Buildings** layer displays some buildings very dramatically, as Google Earth can display both simple and photo-realistic 3D buildings. It only works in some cities, but London is one of them. Try Canary Wharf, or the Houses of Parliament.

Street View

In the latest version of Google Earth (4.3) all of the Street View panorama photos from Google Maps became available as a Google Earth layer. To use it you have to make sure the **Street View** layer is checked in the **Layers** panel.

Street View has been stirring up some controversy in Europe lately. Google have equipped hundreds of cars with a pod on the roof containing eight cameras. These are driving all over Europe taking full panoramic 3D digital images of everything and everybody. But before going any further we suggest you read our Street View coverage of Google Maps, from Page 192. There is no point us repeating the same information.

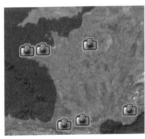

Fig. 14.9 Street View Coverage in France

When an area covered by Street View is present in Google Earth's 3D viewer, camera icons appear as you zoom in closer than 5000 miles. When you double-click one of these, Google Earth zooms in to that location, first showing a semi-transparent sphere, or bubble, on the ground, and then going inside the sphere to open Street View, as shown in **G62**. This really is a very melo-dramatic entry, to say the least.

There are a few differences between Street View in Google Earth and in Google Maps. First, when you press the up or down keys (on the keyboard), the camera tilts up or down, you don't drive down the street. To drive down the street, you double-click another camera icon. To zoom in and out you scroll the mouse wheel (if you have one) up and down. You can also double-click the left mouse button to zoom in, but there is no Zoom Out button as in Google Maps, so you have to use the **Zoom** control buttons in the top-right of the window. With Google Earth you seem to be able to zoom in much further than with Google Maps.

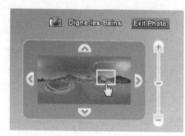

Fig. 14.10 Street View Controls

In Google Earth you can use the controls shown here to zoom or move in Street View. They only appear when you move the mouse pointer over the top-right corner of the 3D viewer.

The image in the middle of the arrows shows you a 2D version of the 3D Street View panorama you are viewing. Clicking any of the buttons around it will move the white box (your current view) around the Street View. You can also drag the white box. The **+** and **–** slider zooms the camera in and out. The **Exit Photo** button takes you out of Street View and back into normal Google Earth.

Keep your eyes open, as Street View will soon be available down your street, if it isn't already. It can be very time consuming, and you probably won't recognise your neighbour as her face will be all blurred out.

Google Sky

Since version 4.2, Google Earth has included a **Google Sky** feature in which you can see a view of the night sky and explore the stars, constellations, galaxies, planets and the moon from your computer. Thanks to partners such as the Hubble Space Telescope, you can see superb imagery of space.

To have a look at these objects in the 3D viewer, click the **Sky** button 🖉. The view you see in Sky is the one above your last location in Google Earth. We are not astronomers and we don't have much more space, so we will leave it to you to explore this feature further. Make sure you have a look in the **Layers** panel to see the features you can turn on and off in Sky.

Some General Comments

Overall as you may have gathered, we think Google Earth is a lot of fun. It's fantastic as an educational tool to let children (both young and old) explore the World. If you are interested, it has a fantastic community, and it makes planning road trips and vacations much easier. If you like looking at and using maps and enjoy your computer, Google Earth is definitely for you.

Image Quality

Google gets the images from satellite and aerial photos, which they then 'stitch together' to make what you see in Google Earth. Sometimes the images themselves are of varying quality. Larger cities are usually sharp and in-focus, but more remote areas can be pretty poor. But they are getting better all the time. There are often dark and light patches marking different aerial image areas.

Now that the images are stamped at the bottom of the screen with their approximate date you can see that some of the photography is quite old.

The image stitching technique sometimes leaves problems with accuracy. Road overlays and labels often look like they are a little out of place. So it is not surgically precise, but it's free after all.

Google Moon

Google has teamed up with scientists at NASA and produced Google Moon, an exciting way to explore the moon and the story of the Apollo missions. It is not actually part of Google Earth but uses the same features. You can access it at **http://www.google.com/moon**. The home page is shown open in colour in the Google Chrome browser in **G63**. Google Moon includes:

A mosaic of black-and-white images prepared by the USGS of what you would see if you were in a lunar orbit.

A lunar terrain map generated by the USGS.

A collection of placemarks that tell the story of the Apollo missions that landed on the moon, an example of which is in Fig. 14.11 below.

A collection of geological and topographic charts of various regions of the moon.

Fig. 14.11 Part of the Apollo 12 Mission to the Moon

If you find the Moon and Sky features of Google Earth of interest, you may like to know they are now also available in your Web browser at http://www.google.com/sky. There is also a section on the planet Mars. Someone at Google is well into space exploration!

15

Google Chrome

 While we were preparing this book, Google launched their new open-source Web browser, called **Chrome**. Google Chrome is designed to be fast, and to cope with the next generation of Web applications that rely heavily on graphics and multimedia, and maybe to compete head on with Internet Explorer and Firefox. It makes an ideal platform for Web applications, such as Google Docs, Gmail and Google Maps which may soon be replacing the software on your computer, if it hasn't already.

Fig. 15.1 The Clean Lines of Google Chrome

Chrome is only currently available for Windows XP (Service Pack 2 or later) and Windows Vista. Being open-source, its code is available for other developers to share. Google have, in fact, borrowed liberally from other open-source browser code, such as Apple, Firefox and even Microsoft's Explorer.

Installing Chrome

Before you can use Chrome you first have to download and install it. Don't worry though, we have found this a painless process on all our computers so far. To install the Windows version, visit **http://www.google.com/chrome** and click the **Download Google Chrome** button.

©2008 Google - Home - About Google - Privacy Policy - Help

Fig. 15.2 Downloading Google Chrome

Read the Terms of Service, then click the **Accept and Install** button to start the procedure. In the background, Google Update will first be installed (unless you already have it). This is then used to download Google Chrome and Gears and install them on your computer. In the future, Google Update will regularly check to see if an update is available for Chrome and silently update you to the newest version.

All you see of the process is the very colourful information window shown in **G64**, followed by the **Welcome to Google Chrome** box (Fig. 15.3). Click the **Start Google Chrome** button to finish the default installation or click the **Customize these settings** link to choose specific installation options.

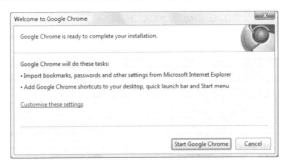

Fig. 15.3 Welcome to Google Chrome

If you want to import your settings from Firefox, you should first close all open Firefox windows. When the process completes, Chrome opens automatically, as shown in Fig. 15.4 below. This may be a good time to click on the **Getting Started page** link to learn about Chrome's features.

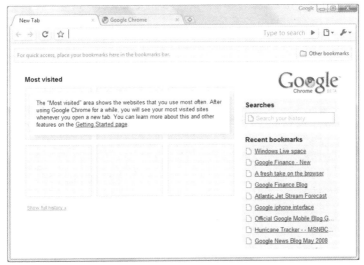

Fig. 15.4 An Empty Chrome New Tab Home Page

By default the **New Tab** page is set as Chrome's home page and opens whenever you start the program, but this is the only time you will see it looking like this. The next time it opens with Chrome, or when you click the ⊕ **New Tab** button, it will have thumbnails of your most visited sites, as we show in colour in **G65**. If you don't like the idea of being presented with evidence of how 'you have wasted your time' every time your browser opens, it is easy to change this, as we explain later. If you click the Google Chrome tab you should get a welcome page similar to **G66**.

As with all Windows applications, you close Chrome by clicking the **Close** button at the top-right of the window, or with the **Alt+F4** keyboard shortcut.

 To open Chrome in the future, you can double-click on the shortcut icon, shown here, that was placed on your desktop during the installation. Google Chrome An easier method is to click the **Google Chrome** button , that was also added to your **Quick Launch** bar (on the left of the Taskbar at the bottom of your screen) when Chrome was installed. With this method you don't have to clear your Desktop to find the button.

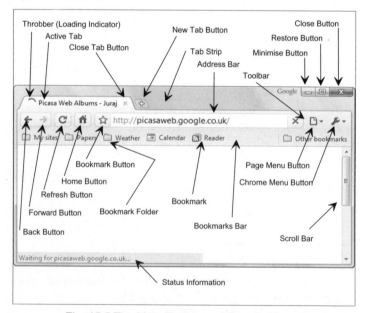

Fig. 15.5 The Main Features of Google Chrome

The Chrome Environment

Fig. 15.5 facing, shows a typical view of the main features of the Google Chrome browser. In fact it shows how we have ours set up for Web browsing. As you can see, it has a clean uncluttered look. Please don't forget that we only have the beta version to work with. The final version may be different.

Tabbed Browsing

Chrome uses tabbed browsing and places opened Web pages in separate tabs on the **Tab Strip** at the top of the window. Google have done away with the usual Title Bar, so unfortunately you don't get a page title at the top.

Fig. 15.6 Loading Indicator

When you load a Web page in a tab, ' Throbber' a slow-spinning grey circle in the favicon area of the tab lets you know that Chrome is connecting. It turns blue and spins faster once loading is actually in progress. When the page has completely loaded, the icon changes to the Web site's favicon graphic (if it has one), as shown in the sequence of Fig. 15.6. While loading, status information also appears in a shaded box at the bottom left of your browser window. When you download a file, an arrow appears on the tab to signify a file download is in progress.

When you open a new tab by clicking the ⊕ **New Tab** button it is placed as the last tab, but you can drag it anywhere else in the Tab Strip. You can drag tabs from the browser window to another window, or to a new window.

To close a tab, click the × icon in the tab, or click the mouse scroll button in it, (or use **Ctrl+W**). In Chrome, each tab operates independently, so if one tab stops working it shouldn't affect any other tabs or Chrome itself.

The Address Bar

In Chrome, you can get anywhere on the Web from one box, the **Address Bar**. Google has combined the **Search** bar and the **Address** bar into one very clever text entry box placed in the middle of its **Toolbar**. You can also use it to bookmark Web pages and check the security of a page.

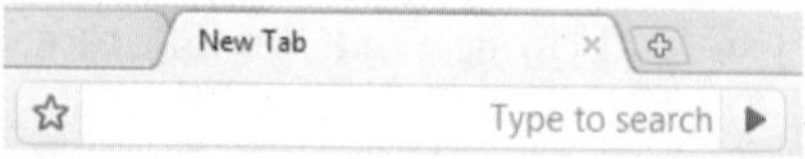

Fig. 15.7 The Address Bar

To make a search you don't have to go to a Google page, just type your search query in the Address Bar, and it will suggest related queries and popular Web sites, based on the text you are typing in.

If you know the URL (Web address) for the site you want to access, type it straight into the Address Bar and press the **Enter** key, or click the arrow icon ▶ to load the page. As you type, Chrome searches your browsing history, as well as its own list of popular Web sites, and gives you matches at the bottom of its drop-down menu, as shown in Fig. 15.8.

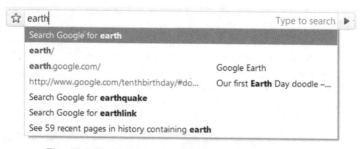

Fig. 15.8 Typical Address Bar Suggestions in Chrome

As you are entering text in the bar, keep your eyes on the drop-down suggestions. If one is what you want, just selecting it will take you straight there. This takes a little getting used to, but it really is a good feature. As you use it more and more the list of suggestions should get better too.

We often copy URLs (with **Ctrl+C**) and paste them into our browser to save typing. Chrome has an even better option

here, you can right-click the Address Bar, and select the
Paste and go option from the context menu, to quickly open
the Web page. You don't even need to select what is already
there.

When loading a Web page, the arrow icon ▶ at the end of
the Address Bar turns into an ✕, which you can click to stop
the loading process.

Bookmarks

In Chrome, your **Bookmarks** (Favorites for Explorer users)
are usually kept on the Bookmarks Bar just below the
Toolbar. Unfortunately, at the moment, there isn't a way of
accessing your Google Toolbar Bookmarks (see page 43),
but we expect that will come in a later version.

The **Ctrl+B** shortcut hides or displays the Bookmarks Bar,
so if you can't see it anywhere, look on the New Tab page
and press **Ctrl+B**, to open the bar as shown in Fig. 15.9.

Fig. 15.9 The Bookmarks Bar when Chrome First Starts

Any imported bookmarks during the installation will have
been placed in one long list in the **Other bookmarks** folder,
shown above. You can organise these by creating new
folders on the bar and dragging bookmarks from one folder to
another. To create a new folder, right-click the Bookmarks
Bar, and select **Add folder**. Type the folder's name in the
New folder box and click the **OK** button. You can nest
folders in the same way.

Fig. 15.10 The
Bookmark Bubble

To bookmark a Web page so
that you can easily access it
again, click the star icon ☆ on
the Chrome toolbar, complete the
Bookmark 'bubble' and click the
Close button. Clicking the
Remove link will cancel the
operation.

Fig. 15.5 shows our Bookmarks Bar. It has several folders and a couple of well used bookmarks on the bar itself. Everything else is stored in the **Other bookmarks** folder.

The Toolbar

The rest of the Chrome Toolbar consists of buttons to help with your browsing and to control Chrome's settings.

The **Forward** and **Back** buttons let you move between different pages you have visited from the current tab. If you click and hold either of the buttons you will see a drop-down menu of more pages from your current browsing session. **Show Full History** will access the History page, listing the Web pages visited with Chrome whilst in standard mode.

Fig. 15.11

The **Refresh** button which reloads the current Web page.

The **Home** button returns Chrome to the current home page. You can set your home page in the **Options** section of the **Tools** 🔧▾ menu, shown below. This button does not show by default, but is so useful we have shown it selected.

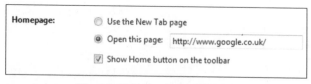

Fig. 15.12 Home Page Options

The **Page Control** button opens a drop-down menu (Fig. 15.18) with options often seen on the menu bar of other browsers. These include tab controls, **Cut, Copy, Paste**, **Find in page**, **Save page as**, **Print**, **Text zoom** and other development type options.

The **Tools Menu** button opens a drop-down menu of options to customise and control Chrome, as shown here.

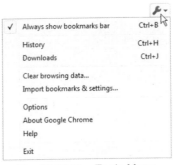

Most of these are fairly self explanatory. Probably the two most important ones being **Help** and **Options**.

Fig. 15.13 The Tools Menu

Help opens Chrome's Help System, which for Google, is quite extensive. You will probably need to work your way through this later.

Options opens the dialogue box shown in Fig. 15.14. Here is where you set the **Homepage**, what appears in Chrome at start up and the Searching and browsing defaults.

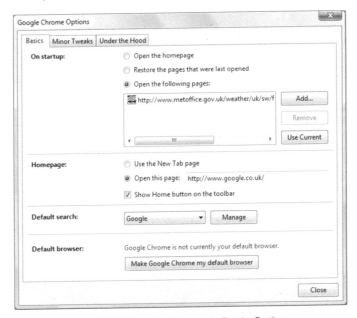

Fig. 15.14 Google Chrome's Basic Options

Clicking the Minor Tweaks tab opens another settings page.

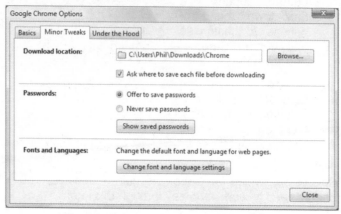

Fig. 15.15 Chrome's Minor Tweaks Options

The Under the Hood tab opens yet another settings page.

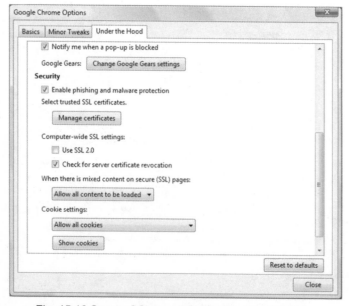

Fig. 15.16 Some of Chrome's Under the Hood Options

Incognito Mode

There may be times that we all want to browse in stealth mode, perhaps to plan something we don't want other people that use our computer to know about, or just to view more borderline areas of the Internet. In Chrome you do this in a window set to '**Incognito Mode**'. In this mode, Web pages you open and files you download are not recorded in Chrome's history, and any new cookies are deleted after you close the incognito window.

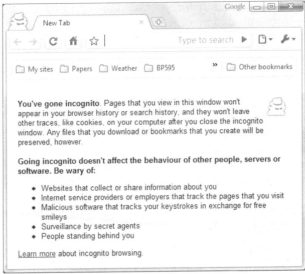

Fig. 15.17 Opening a New Tab in Incognito Mode

To turn on incognito mode, click the **Page menu** button and select **New incognito window** from the drop-down menu. A new window will open with the incognito icon in the top left corner, as shown in Fig. 15.17 above. You can also right-click a link on a Web page and select **Open link in incognito window**.

When the 'spy' icon is active you can safely browse without leaving any traces. Just closing the incognito window returns Chrome to standard mode. You cannot drag between incognito and standard mode windows.

Application Windows

As we have seen in earlier chapters, many Web site applications like Gmail, Google Calendar and Google Docs, operate like actual programs that are installed on your computer. Chrome supports these Web applications by providing a special window designed for them.

The procedure is that you first create an **Application Shortcut** for the online application on your desktop. Then you can open the application in a special window, by double-clicking the desktop shortcut.

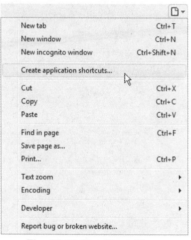

We will use our Google Calendar as an example of this. With the Calendar open in Chrome, click the **Page menu** button 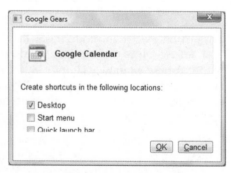 and select **Create application shortcuts** as shown here in Fig. 15.18.

Fig. 15.18 The Page Menu

In the **Google Gears** box that opens, you select where you want shortcuts to be placed on your computer. In our case we only want one on the **Desktop**, but you can also have them in the **Start menu** and the **Quick launch bar**.

Click the **OK** button to place the shortcut as shown on the facing page.

Fig. 15.19 The Google Gears Box

Google
Calendar

When you double-click an application shortcut, the Web site opens in its own Google Chrome window with as much working room as possible.

Fig. 15.20 Google Calendar in its Own Application Window

As can be seen in Fig. 15.20 above, application windows don't have tabs, buttons or an address bar. If you need any navigation or Web page functions, you can click the **Logo** button in the top-left of the window (in our example above) to open a drop-down menu of options.

While working in the Web application, if you click on a link that takes you to a different Web site, it will open in a new Chrome window, and your application will remain intact.

This feature makes working with applications like Google Docs very much easier. Unfortunately it was not available when we were preparing the chapters on the Google Applications.

Downloading Files

You probably know that to download a photograph from a Web page, you right-click it and select the **Save image as** option and choose a saving location.

Fig. 15.21 Saving a Photograph from a Web Page in Chrome

With Chrome, when the download starts a large blue down-arrow briefly appears pointing to a download file button in the bottom left of the Chrome window, as shown in Fig. 15.21 above.

When the download is complete, you can drag the new file from the button to the Desktop or another folder, you can click the button to open it, or click the arrow beside the button

Fig. 15.22 Downloaded File Options

for more options, as shown below.

To see all your downloads, click the **Show all downloads** link (Fig. 15.21). You can also view details of all your downloads by opening the **Tools** 🔧▾ menu and selecting **Downloads** (or use the **Ctrl+J** shortcut).

Security in Chrome

If Chrome detects that the Web site you are trying to access will securely transmit data using SSL, you should see the following features in the Address Bar.

Fig. 15.23 The Address Bar for a Secure Transaction

The background colour of the address bar should change to gold, and the **https** part of the address (in the URL) should appear in green if a secure SSL connection has been established. A lock icon 🔒 should also show at the right end of the address bar. All of these are shown in Fig. 15.23 above. This all shows you should have a secure connection and can safely transact your business. If a secure connection can't be made you should see an alert icon ⚠ at the end of the address bar, which you can click to see what the problem is.

With its default settings, Chrome also has security measures in place to help protect you as you browse the Web. As long as **Phishing and malware protection** is enabled (see Fig. 15.16), Google downloads to your browser a list of information about sites that may contain malicious software or engage in phishing. Your computer can then check if you are visiting a risky site, and warn you, as below.

Fig. 15.24 A Very Strong Warning not to Visit a Web Site

Cookies are files created on your computer by many Web sites you visit. They store information, such as your preferences for that particular site. You should be aware of your cookie settings as they can allow Web sites to track your navigation during your visit to a site. In Chrome you can adjust the level of permission for cookies in the **Security** section opened by clicking the **Tools menu** 🔧 ▾ button and selecting **Options, Under the Hood** (Fig. 15.16).

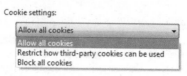

Fig. 15.25 Setting the Protection Level for Cookies

We strongly recommend you leave Chrome's other security settings as they are, unless you are very sure of yourself.

* * *

We have tried to cover the parts of Google Chrome that make it special as a browser. We have been impressed with its simplicity, performance and speed. It really is a pleasure to use. At the time of writing it was still in beta version, but we found it remarkably robust. By the time you read this the full version will probably have been released, and most of the 'missing' features will have been added.

One of the exciting things about writing this book was the speed with which things change with Google. Nothing seems to stay the same for long.

We hope you enjoy the book, we certainly enjoyed the research involved. Hopefully there may be enough demand for a follow up, in the not too distant future.

Appendix A

Google Calculator Reference

The calculator can evaluate mathematical expressions involving basic arithmetic, advanced math, units of measure and conversions, and physical constants.

Basic Arithmetic

The following table lists operators that come between the two numbers on which they operate, e.g., to multiply 2 times 3, use 2 * 3.

Operator	Function
+	Addition [15.99 + 32.50 + 13.25]
−	Subtraction [79 − 18 − 19]
*	Multiplication [2 * 3 * 7]
/	Division [378 / 9]
^	Exponentiation (raise to a power of) [4^10]
% of	Percentage [15% of 93.45]
mod or %	Modulo (the remainder after division) [15 mod 9] or [15 % 9]
nth root of	Calculates the nth root [4th root of 16]; [cube root of 109]; [square root of 42] or [sqrt(42)]

Advanced Maths

Calculates results involving mathematical constants, such as e, pi, i (the square root of −1), and other mathematical functions such as:

Trigonometric Functions (arguments are assumed to be in radians)

sin	Sine [eg. sin(pi/6)]
cos	Cosine

tan	Tangent
sec	Secant
csc	Cosecant
cot	Cotangent

Inverse Trigonometric Functions

arcsin	Arcsine
arccos	Arccosine
arctan	Arctangent
arccsc	Arccosecant

Hyperbolic Functions

sinh	Sinh – Hyperbolic sine of a number.
cosh	Cosh – Hyperbolic cosine.
tanh	Tanh – Hyperbolic tangent.
csch	Csch – Hyperbolic cosecant.
arsinh	Arsinh – Inverse hyperbolic sine.
arccsch	Arccsch – Inverse hyperbolic cosine.

Logarithmic Functions

Ln	Natural logarithm to the base e. [eg. ln(16)].
Log	Common logarithm to the base 10.
Lg	Binary logarithm to the base 2.
Exp	Exponential function, used to be called antilog.
!	Factorial function. [eg. 5!]

Mathematical Constants

These are some of the physical constants built into the calculator.

Name	Description
e	base of the natural system of logarithms [eg. e]
pi	The ratio of the circumference to the diameter of a circle [eg. pi/6]
i	Imaginary number, which represents one of the two square roots of −1 [eg. i^2]
gamma	Euler's constant [eg. e^gamma]

Units of Measure and Conversions

The calculator can work with expressions using different units. By default, units are converted to and results expressed in *mks* units. When units have both long and short names you can use either. To make a conversion, use the expression **in** in the query. **1976 in roman numerals** for example.

Type	Examples of Units Used
Currency	Australian Dollars (AUD), British pounds (GBP), Euros, US Dollars (USD)
Mass	kilogram or kg, grams or g, grains, pounds or lbs, carats, stones, tons, tonnes
Length	meters or m, miles, feet, Angstroms, cubits, furlongs
Volume	gallons, liters or l, bushels, teaspoons, pints
Area	square kilometers, acres, hectares
Time	days, seconds or s, centuries, sidereal years, fortnights
Electricity	volts, amps, ohms, henrys (inductance).
Energy	Calories, British thermal units (BTU), joules, ergs, foot-pounds
Power	watt, kilowatts, horsepower or hp
Data	bits, bytes, kbytes, etc.
Quantity	dozen, baker's dozen, percent, gross, great gross, score, googol

Numbering Systems

The numbering systems that can be used include:

decimal, hexadecimal or hex, octal, binary, and roman numerals.

You prefix hexadecimal numbers with 0x, octal numbers with 0o and binary numbers with 0b.

Physical Constants

The following table lists many of the 'commonly' used physical constants built into the calculator function. You can use short names, when they are available, or type the full long names.

Long Name	Short Name
atomic mass units	amu
Astronomical Unit	au
Avogadro's number	
Boltzmann's constant	k
electric constant	
electron mass	m_e
electron volt	eV
elementary charge	
Euler's constant	
Faraday constant	
fine-structure constant	
gravitational constant	G
magnetic flux quantum	
mass of planets	m_mars or m_earth...
mass of the sun	m_sun
molar gas constant	
permeability of free space	
Planck's constant	h
proton mass	m_p
radius of planets	r_earth or r_pluto...
radius of the sun	r_sun
Rydberg constant	
speed of light in a vacuum	c
speed of sound in air at sea level	
Stefan-Boltzmann constant	

Appendix B

Google Finance Sources

The International exchanges and indices covered by Google Finance, with their respective time delays.

Exchange	Delay
American Stock Exchange	20 min
Australian Stock Exchange	20 min
Bank of Canada	15 min
Bombay Stock Exchange	10 min
Canadian Venture Exchange	15 min
Commodity Systems, Inc.	End-of-Day
Dow Jones Indices	Real-time
Euronext: Amsterdam	15 min
Euronext: Brussels	15 min
Euronext: Lisbon	15 min
Euronext: Paris	15 min
FTSE Indices	15 min
Hong Kong Stock Exchange	15 min
London Stock Exchange (LSE)	20 min
Milan Stock Exchange	20 min
NASDAQ Indices	Real-time
NASDAQ Stock Exchange	Real-time
New York Stock Exchange	Real-time
New York Stock Exchange Indices	Real-time
New Zealand Stock Exchange	20 min
S&P Indices	Real-time
Shanghai Stock Exchange	Real-time
Shenzhen Stock Exchange	Real-time
Taiwan Stock Exchange	20 min
Telekurs	End-of-Day
Toronto Stock Exchange	15 min

Index